Advancing Equitable Decisionmaking for the Department of Defense Through Fairness in Machine Learning

IRINEO CABREROS, JOSHUA SNOKE, OSONDE A. OSOBA, INEZ KHAN, MARC N. ELLIOTT

For more information on this publication, visit **www.rand.org/t/RRA1542-1**.

About RAND

The RAND Corporation is a research organization that develops solutions to public policy challenges to help make communities throughout the world safer and more secure, healthier and more prosperous. RAND is nonprofit, nonpartisan, and committed to the public interest. To learn more about RAND, visit www.rand.org.

Research Integrity

Our mission to help improve policy and decisionmaking through research and analysis is enabled through our core values of quality and objectivity and our unwavering commitment to the highest level of integrity and ethical behavior. To help ensure our research and analysis are rigorous, objective, and nonpartisan, we subject our research publications to a robust and exacting quality-assurance process; avoid both the appearance and reality of financial and other conflicts of interest through staff training, project screening, and a policy of mandatory disclosure; and pursue transparency in our research engagements through our commitment to the open publication of our research findings and recommendations, disclosure of the source of funding of published research, and policies to ensure intellectual independence. For more information, visit www.rand.org/about/research-integrity.

RAND's publications do not necessarily reflect the opinions of its research clients and sponsors.

Published by the RAND Corporation, Santa Monica, Calif.
© 2023 RAND Corporation
RAND® is a registered trademark.

Library of Congress Cataloging-in-Publication Data is available for this publication.
ISBN: 978-1-9774-1025-2

Cover: ArtHead/iStock/Getty Images Plus.

About This Report

There is growing concern that machine learning (ML) algorithms can reinforce or exacerbate racial biases in the many sectors in which these algorithms are applied. The U.S. Department of Defense (DoD) is investing in the development of ML methods to assist a wide array of decisions. If the possibility for algorithmic bias is not anticipated and addressed, discriminatory practices analogous to those observed in other sectors may be repeated in DoD. In this report, we aim to provide developers of ML algorithms for DoD with a framework and tools to develop equitable algorithms. We propose a process for developing algorithms that are consistent with DoD's equity priorities. We also introduce the RAND Algorithmic Equity Tool, which allows algorithm developers to enforce equity constraints on predictive algorithms while assessing the inherent trade-offs to doing so. The research reported here was conducted as part of a RAND Project AIR FORCE (PAF) initiative to support diversity, equity, and inclusion (DEI) within the Department of the Air Force. Oversight of the initiative was provided by Dr. Ray Conley.

RAND Project AIR FORCE

RAND Project AIR FORCE (PAF), a division of the RAND Corporation, is the Department of the Air Force's (DAF's) federally funded research and development center for studies and analyses, supporting both the United States Air Force and the United States Space Force. PAF provides the DAF with independent analyses of policy alternatives affecting the development, employment, combat readiness, and support of current and future air, space, and cyber forces. Research is conducted in four programs: Strategy and Doctrine; Force Modernization and Employment; Resource Management; and Workforce, Development, and Health. The research reported here was prepared under contract FA7014-16-D-1000.

Additional information about PAF is available on our website:
www.rand.org/paf/

The draft report, issued on August 16, 2021, was reviewed by formal peer reviewers and DAF subject-matter experts.

Funding

Funding for this research was made possible by the independent research and development provisions of RAND's contracts for the operation of its U.S. Department of Defense federally funded research and development centers.

Acknowledgments

Inez Khan, Irineo Cabreros, and Joshua Snoke were responsible for the development and production of the accompanying RAND Algorithmic Equity Tool. We would like to acknowledge the RAND Corporation and the RAND Initiated Research program for funding that supported this project and the development of this report. We thank the leadership and guidance from Susan Marquis, Lisa Jaycox, and Ray Conley in the development of this report. We thank Benjamin Boudreaux and Paul Emslie for their careful review and comments that have strengthened the report, and we thank Rebecca Weir and Hansell Perez for reviewing the tool. We received feedback and input from many individuals who helped move these ideas forward and develop the concepts in this report. In this respect, we would like to particularly thank David Schulker, Lisa Harrington, Molly McIntosh, Jeannette Haynie, Lou Mariano, Nelson Lim, and the RAND Statistics Group.

Contents

Figures and Tables

Figures

Tables

Summary

Issue

Machine learning (ML) algorithms are increasingly used as an aid to human decisionmaking. However, there is a growing recognition that the use of ML algorithms may reinforce or exacerbate human biases, thereby perpetuating inequities. This situation is commonly referred to as *algorithmic bias*. The U.S. Department of Defense (DoD) is investing heavily in the development of ML algorithms to assist in many decisionmaking processes. At the same time, DoD has a strong stated interest in promoting diversity, equity, and inclusion (DE&I) at all levels of the organization. The goal of this report is to provide policymakers and developers of ML algorithms with a framework and tools to produce algorithms that are consistent with DoD's equity priorities. This report represents part of a larger effort to advance equity in DoD.

Although predictive ML algorithms are deployed in some sectors within DoD—including intelligence and surveillance—ML algorithms are in the preliminary stages of development and are not at this time deployed in decisionmaking processes in the personnel space, where DoD has expressed equity goals. Despite this, we observe a growing interest in using ML algorithms as part of personnel decisions, as evidenced by the prototype tools developed in this space. Therefore, the utility of this report is primarily to preempt the possibility of algorithmic bias in eventual personnel decisionmaking applications within DoD rather than to address existing instances of algorithmic bias.

Approach

We provide a review of the written DoD policies and statements regarding DE&I in order to understand DoD's equity goals. We provide examples of the active development of ML technologies that interact with these equity goals, focusing specifically on ML algorithms that are embedded in decisionmaking processes. We review the technical concepts of algorithmic fairness and draw connections between DoD policy equity goals and possible comparable technical definitions of equity. We do not critique DoD policy statements as part of this work, though additional work could consider the adequacy of DoD's policies.

We developed a framework and software tool, the RAND Algorithmic Equity Tool, to assist in the development of equitable predictive algorithms.[1] For binary classification algorithms, this tool allows users to modify an algorithm to enforce specified equity goals. It also allows users to modify input training data to minimize the predictive influence of a protected

---

[1] The tool is an interactive online RShiny application, which can be accessed on the product page for this report (www.rand.org/t/RRA1542-1).

attribute, such as race or sex. Importantly, the RAND Algorithmic Equity Tool helps users visualize trade-offs that are inherent to enforcing equity, such as diminished predictive accuracy. We display the functionality of this tool using a hypothetical ML algorithm that informs promotion decisions by automatically scoring candidates based on performance reviews, and we use the tool to enforce definitions of equity that may meet DoD's policy goals.

Conclusions

With respect to DoD's equity goals, we identify three principles that may be linked to mathematical notions of equity: (1) career entry and progression should be free of discrimination with respect to protected attributes, including race, religion, or sex, (2) career placement and progression within DoD should be based on merit, and (3) DoD should represent the demographics of the country it serves. We argue that each of these principles corresponds to a notion of algorithmic fairness: specifically, *fairness through unawareness*, *true positive rate balance*, and *statistical parity*, respectively.

To aid the development of equitable algorithms for particular decisionmaking processes, we propose the following five-stage procedure:

1. Determine equity risk.
2. Identify relevant equity mandates and priorities.
3. Determine relevant equity definitions.
4. Identify important performance priorities.
5. Weigh trade-offs of enforcing equity.

We show in our theoretical case study how this framework could be used to constrain algorithms to meet the identified DoD principles and the possible trade-offs with such constraints. In practice, it is not possible to satisfy each principle simultaneously, so priorities will need to be set. In our application of the RAND Algorithmic Equity Tool to a hypothetical case study, we show what it may look like to successfully enforce equity priorities.

Recommendations

Although ML algorithms have the potential to simplify existing human decisionmaking processes, there is a need to audit them to ensure that they do not result in inequitable outcomes. However, there is no universal approach to defining equitable outcomes; different decisionmaking processes involve different equity concerns. Additionally, attaining equity can come at the cost of other important priorities.

Therefore, the framework we recommend for developing equitable ML algorithms requires precisely defined equity and non-equity priorities. We emphasize that this required degree of precision is seldom available in the official mandates and statements provided by DoD regarding its DE&I priorities. To facilitate the development of equitable ML algorithms, DoD should collaborate with experts in the field of algorithmic fairness to translate institutional equity priorities into mathematical definitions. Once precise equity priorities are defined, the RAND Algorithmic Equity Tool allows users to enforce equity goals while monitoring the necessary trade-offs.

We propose that algorithms can and should be used as aids to human decisionmaking processes, both because algorithms can help reduce subjective human bias and because it is easier to audit and alter a well-constructed algorithm to enforce equitable outcomes. Although this report focuses on auditing algorithms, non-algorithmic (human only) processes can be similarly audited to ensure they are equitable. The findings in this report should be useful for framing the idea of equity, determining how to measure fairness, and collecting the right information in order to audit decisionmaking processes.

Abbreviations

AI	artificial intelligence
DBDI	DoD Board on Diversity and Inclusion
DE&I	diversity, equity, and inclusion
DoD	U.S. Department of Defense
EEOC	Equal Employment Opportunity Commission
JAIC	Joint Artificial Intelligence Center
ML	machine learning
USD(P&R)	Under Secretary of Defense for Personnel and Readiness

CHAPTER ONE

Introduction

There is a growing recognition that machine learning (ML) algorithms can perpetuate or exacerbate inequities. This situation, which is commonly referred to as *algorithmic bias*, has been observed in many domains in which ML algorithms are used to assist in decisionmaking processes, including criminal justice, health care, insurance industries, and hiring practices. Algorithmic bias runs counter to the intuition that algorithms can provide objective measures that are free from the subjectivity and bias of a human decisionmaking process. This bias often occurs when ML algorithms are designed to predict outcomes using historical data, inadvertently recapitulating human biases rather than eliminating them.

The U.S. Department of Defense (DoD) is investing heavily in the development of ML technologies to assist many decisionmaking processes in a variety of capacities. At the same time, DoD has expressed a strong commitment to promoting diversity, equity, and inclusion (DE&I) across the organization. The purpose of this report is to provide guidance and tools to enable the production of ML algorithms that are in line with DoD's stated equity priorities. This report focuses on algorithms to support personnel management decisions, for which there are both stated equity goals and interest in using ML algorithms to assist decisionmaking. Nonpersonnel algorithmic applications, such as autonomous weapons systems or surveillance technologies, can also raise significant equity concerns. However, we do not explore these applications in this report.

In Chapter Two, we provide an overview of the equity priorities of DoD through its official policies and statements. These priorities largely relate to the management of personnel, through recruitment, retention, and promotion policies. We identify three central equity principles that guide DoD's personnel priorities. First, individuals should have equal opportunity, and processes should be free from discriminatory prejudice with respect to protected characteristics, such as race, religion, or sex. Second, DoD is a meritocracy, and career placement and progression within DoD should be based on merit. Third, the demographic composition of DoD should reflect the nation that it serves.

In Chapter Three, we summarize DoD's investment in ML. Although DoD uses ML technologies in several sectors (e.g., in intelligence and surveillance), we find that DoD does not currently rely on ML technologies in personnel management. Therefore, we view this report as primarily preemptive. In Chapter Three, we review ML technologies that have been developed (although not deployed) to assist in decisionmaking processes regarding personnel, where DoD's equity goals are focused.

In Chapter Four, we review some of the central concepts of the algorithmic fairness literature. There are three important lessons from this literature that guide our proposed framework and tool for developing equitable ML algorithms. First, there are many definitions of equity, each with subtly different implications. Second, it is generally not possible to attain multiple types of equity simultaneously. It is typically the case that attaining one form of equity necessitates violating another. Therefore, it is important to be targeted when defining equity priorities. Finally, enforcing an algorithm to behave equitably typically comes at the cost of other performance priorities, such as overall predictive accuracy.

In Chapter Five, we propose a five-step framework for developing equitable ML algorithms. The first step is to determine the equity risk posed by the ML application in question. We emphasize that not all ML algorithms pose an imminent risk to equity. In particular, algorithms that do not assist in decisionmaking processes that affect individuals may not need to be evaluated from an equity lens. If the algorithm in question does pose an equity risk, one then proceeds to the second step, which is to determine the equity priorities surrounding the decisionmaking process that the ML algorithm is assisting. These equity priorities are then translated into mathematical expressions of equity, which is the third step of our framework. Because equity interventions may come at a cost to other performance priorities, the fourth step is to define the non-equity priorities of the algorithm. In most cases, overall predictive accuracy will be an important performance priority, which is not directly related to equity. The final step of the framework is to weigh the trade-offs of enforcing equity. This step is assisted by the RAND Algorithmic Equity Tool, which is provided as an interactive online RShiny application.[1] This tool allows the user to modify a predictive algorithm to behave more equitably while displaying the trade-offs inherent to doing so.

After overviewing the overall structure of our equity framework, we walk through this framework in Chapter Six using a hypothetical case study. In this case study, we evaluate a hypothetical algorithm used to assist promotion selection decisions by providing an automated score for candidates. We show how to use the RAND Algorithmic Equity Tool to identify modifications to the original algorithm that enforce relevant equity priorities while measuring the effect on algorithmic performance. Finally, we provide concluding recommendations in Chapter Seven.

---

[1] The tool is an interactive online RShiny application, which can be accessed on the product page for this report (www.rand.org/t/RRA1542-1).

CHAPTER TWO

The Department of Defense's Investment in Equity

DoD has a growing interest in measuring and enhancing DE&I. In recent years, DoD, along with the Department of the Air Force, Department of the Navy, and Department of the Army, have released directives and policies on DE&I. This report focuses specifically on DoD personnel management processes and decisions,[1] the most common of which are recruitment, job assignment, promotion, retention, and disciplinary actions.

The steps required to address DE&I matters are multifaceted, and we do not address all aspects in this report. We broadly categorize the types of strategies into the following three groups (these groups are not mutually exclusive but can interact with each other):

1. *assessment* strategies that seek to understand the underlying causes of disparities, which include benchmark and barriers analyses
2. *enabling* strategies that seek to address the culture of an organization through such approaches as leadership engagement on diversity, accountability, and culture changes (such as diversity training)
3. *process* strategies that seek to audit specific decisionmaking processes and, if necessary, change them to mitigate bias and produce equitable decisions.

We adapt this language from Lim, Cho, and Curry Hall, 2008, to highlight the concept of a strategy toward increased diversity and equity. According to them, a policy is defined as a strategy if "it is deliberate and is associated with a bigger picture of where the organization is headed" (Lim, Cho, and Curry Hall, 2008, p. 35). Following their work, we separate *process* strategies from *enabling* strategies. Because of the nature of algorithm-aided decisionmaking, which we discuss in Chapter Three, we focus our work solely on process strategies. Process strategies relate to the operational systems that affect the equity of outcomes for individuals, such as how DoD handles accessions, career assignments, and promotions.

---

[1] DoD's investment in equity and the findings of this report go beyond personnel management, and there are many important equity and ethical questions in regard to, for example, autonomous weapons or surveillance. We address these topics in Appendix C.

We separate out the first category of assessment strategies as distinct from process strategies because a large portion of DE&I work seeks to first understand why we observe disparities and whether the problems are solvable. In some cases, the policy solutions from assessment strategies do not involve altering specific decisionmaking processes. They do not necessarily assume a strategy of addressing cultural or process issues but instead act as a first step to assess the problem. This work carries additional importance in DoD because of the pipeline issue. By this we mean the general idea that, in a personnel pipeline that includes a sequence of decisions, decisions earlier in the pipeline can affect outcomes further down the pipeline. For much of DoD (particularly in the military), individuals are only promoted internally, so disparities at lower ranks typically translate into disparities at higher ranks. In other words, because senior DoD personnel must go through the pipeline, disparities at the upper levels may not be easily reduced until disparities earlier in the pipeline are addressed.

Although enabling strategies and assessment strategies merit attention and at times will overlap with process strategies, this report focuses in particular on DoD's investment in tools to audit and mitigate potential bias in decisionmaking processes in order to achieve more-equitable outcomes.[2] We will not cover enabling or assessment strategies within our scope of recommendations. As we focus on process strategies, we further delineate between strategies that rely on procedural-based equity or those that rely on outcome- or substantive-based equity. As we will show in DoD's equity policies and in the concepts of algorithmic fairness, some processes seek to be equitable by constraining the procedure to be fair, while others seek to be equitable by constraining the outcomes of the process to be fair. Both of these are valid approaches, and we highlight the differences to help better understand what type of equity the process strategy is seeking.

To better understand DoD's investment in equity, we start by reviewing DoD's DE&I policies concerning personnel management, along with some prior work on disparities in DoD and strategies for tackling this issue.

Official Statements on Equity

DoD has made it clear through established policies concerning DE&I that equity is a point of importance alongside the more standard goals of readiness and global competitiveness. In 2012, DoD issued a five-year Diversity and Inclusion Strategy Plan (DoD, 2012) with a focus on defining diversity and laying out a strategy for diversity management. In 2020, the DoD Board on Diversity and Inclusion (DBDI) released a report with 15 specific recommendations (DBDI, 2020), which were later advanced (Miller, 2020). This report outlined more-specific targets for recruitment, retention, and promotion among underrepresented minority

---

[2] In this report, we use the terms *equity* and *fairness* interchangeably. In certain contexts, these terms may have different connotations, but we assume them both to mean equality in a particular outcome of interest for individuals of different groups, such as races. Definitions of different ways to measure equality are discussed in detail in Chapter Three.

groups, with an increased focus on data collection and utilization for informing diversity management. In addition to DoD-wide policies, the Air Force, Army, and Navy have each released guidance on equity and diversity and offer guidance on applications of equal opportunity, nondiscrimination, and diversity (Air Force Instruction 36-7001, 2019; Headquarters, Department of the Army, 2010; U.S. Navy Chief of Naval Operations, 2020).[3] These documents generally refer in broad terms to how equity is defined and will be achieved, and we highlight some specifics here in order to draw out the motivating concepts of equity that are relevant to this report.

The first recommendation from the DBDI report we highlight advises action in increasing diversity and inclusion, particularly in the areas of recruitment, accessions, and retention. Recommendation 1.2 states that the military should develop

> DoD-wide data-driven accessions and retention strategy for officers and enlisted personnel to achieve a talent pipeline reflecting the diversity of the current and future eligible population from U.S. Census projections. (DBDI, 2020, p. ix)

First, this recommendation indicates that DoD has specific numerical goals with regard to diversity, stating that "DoD must monitor current and future demographic population trends in order to measure its own demographics accordingly with the aim of reflecting the nation" (DBDI, 2020, p. 22). Second, the desired state is when "racial and ethnic representation within the military is more consistent across all grades" (DBDI, 2020, p. 22). This goal reiterates a 2011 report that stated a goal of attaining "an officer and enlisted corps across all communities and ranks that reflects the eligible U.S. population" (Military Leadership Diversity Commission, 2011, p. 4). These policy recommendations describe a process that seeks a type of outcome equity.

The Air Force, Army, and Navy documents state similar commitments to achieving a military population that reflects the demographics of the United States. They also emphasize recruitment, retention, and progression through the ranks. The Air Force policy differs somewhat by stating that

> [n]o numerical goals may be set for the hiring or promotion of Air Force military or civilian personnel on the basis of race, color, national origin, religion, sex (including gender identity), age, or sexual orientation. (Air Force Instruction 36-7001, 2019, p. 4)

However, Air Force policy does state that numerical goals are permissible for veterans and other civilians with disabilities and that it is acceptable to set goals for the number of applicants by such characteristics as gender or race. Although these ideas may be implicit in other policies, only the Air Force directive explicitly references numerical goals in any of the policies we reviewed for this report. We note a possible internal tension with the policy that

---

[3] Although we do not exclude them, we do not provide a specific focus on policies or outcomes for DoD civilian personnel or for U.S. Coast Guard personnel working with the Department of Homeland Security.

it is acceptable to set goals for applications although it is not acceptable to set the same goals for accessions or promotions. One interpretation is that these policies implicitly assume that the processes of hiring and promotion are unbiased and that a representative applicant pool is sufficient to achieve a force that reflects the U.S. population.

For the second area we highlight, the DBDI report includes multiple recommendations concerning the promotion process. In addition to ensuring the pipeline is adequately diverse, the DBDI recommends auditing various aspects of the process to mitigate potential bias. Recommendation 1.4 states that the Under Secretary of Defense for Personnel and Readiness (USD[P&R])

> will conduct an initial and biennial assessment of all aptitude tests currently administered by the Military Departments to analyze and remove barriers that adversely impact diversity and are unrelated to predictive validity. (DBDI, 2020, p. ix)

This recommendation stems from a concern that "research demonstrates persistent racial and ethnic gaps in preparation for aptitude tests" (DBDI, 2020, p. 24). Using the Armed Services Vocational Aptitude Batter (ASVAB) test as an example, DBDI notes that "ASVAB scores only tell how well someone is expected to perform relative to others in the youth population rather than predicting an absolute or specific level of performance" (DBDI, 2020, p. 24).

In other words, this recommendation is meant to address the concern that personnel decisions are being made using predictors that affect diversity (e.g., are correlated with such characteristics as race or gender) but do not predict the outcomes of interest for DoD, such as high performance. The goal of this recommendation is to explore alternative methods of predicting performance that maintain high validity but minimize disparity.

There also is an expressed desire to increase the transparency of promotion selection decisionmaking processes. The DBDI's Recommendation 2 advises USD(P&R) to "monitor and evaluate demographic trends in performance evaluations to inform career development processes and identify potential biases in supervisor/rater populations" (DBDI, 2020, p. x).

Similarly, Recommendation 5.4 states that USD(P&R) "will establish procedures for the release of demographic and other contextual data concerning promotion selection board results to improve transparency in career management processes" (DBDI, 2020, p. xi).

Together these recommendations seek to increase the transparency of the performance evaluation and promotion processes and track selection rates with regard to race, ethnicity, and gender. This policy goal reflects a desire for procedural equity.

Among the departments within DoD, a 2021 Navy report builds directly on the DBDI report and, in some cases, extends its recommendations to add more-explicit guidance (Task Force One Navy, 2021). In particular, Recommendation 5.14 suggests that the Navy use artificial intelligence (AI) in its promotion selection decisionmaking pipeline:

> Pilot the use of AI capability for centralized selection boards to support the selection process and minimize bias in the selection process. AI would not replace the human inter-

vention for this process, but rather support processes and potentially serve as a bias mitigation capability. (Task Force One Navy, 2021, p. 31)

This aligns with Recommendation 5.4 from the DBDI report as part of auditing and mitigating potential bias in the promotion process.

The last recommendation from the DBDI report we highlight focuses on the collection of data and metrics to improve DoD's tracking of diversity and equity. Recommendation 4.2 proposes to

> establish an enterprise-wide data system to improve DoD's ability to aggregate Military Department human resource data to perform demographic, diversity, and inclusion analysis on Defense Manpower Data Center (DMDC) data. (DBDI, 2020, p. x)

We also note that language in regard to ensuring equal opportunity is common throughout the directives, similar to equal opportunity policies established by the Equal Employment Opportunity Commission (EEOC) and the U.S. Office of Personnel Management. The civilian and military sides of DoD both have statements regarding equal opportunity that preclude the "unlawful discrimination on the basis of race, color, national origin, religion, sex (including gender identity), or sexual orientation" (Department of Defense Directive 1020.02E, 2018, p. vi).[4]

For an in-depth review of the relationship between DoD's current diversity policies and equal opportunity, we refer readers to Kamarck, 2019.

Prior Research on Disparities in DoD

Prior studies have analyzed disparities in DoD, seeking to both quantify the level of disparities and understand how they arise. We review a few studies here that are connected to the types of personnel disparities that are relevant to the strategies and policies highlighted in the previous sections.

In an extensive report prepared for Congress, Kamarck, 2019, provides findings concerning racial diversity across the whole DoD, finding that racial minorities are overrepresented in the lower ranks but underrepresented among officers and senior leadership. We replicate Table 6 from Kamarck, 2019, in Table 2.1, which shows racial representation by selected levels.

Kamarck, 2019, outlines the historical trends of representation in DoD and the systematic issues faced by racial minorities in participation, promotion, and retention. The report highlights the desire for equity-focused DoD policies to improve diversity and opportunities for minorities, but it also acknowledges the complexity of the issue. This highlights a possible tension between achieving equity goals and achieving other military goals, such as a merit-based system or military readiness. It is notable that Kamarck, 2019, came before the 2020

---

[4] The DoD Civilian Equal Employment Opportunity Program statement includes additional categories not covered by the DoD Military Equal Opportunity Program.

TABLE 2.1

Race and Ethnic Representation in the Active Component and U.S. Population (as of May 2018)

Rank and Grade	White	Black	Asian	American Indian/ Alaska Native	Native Hawaiian/ Pacific Islander	Multi/Unknown	Hispanic[a]
General and flag officer (O-7 and above)	87.5%	8.1%	1.8%	None	0.3%	2.4%	2.1%
Officer (all)	77.3%	8.1%	5.2%	10.1%	0.5%	8.2%	7.6%
Warrant officer	69.0%	16.0%	3.1%	0.8%	0.6%	10.4%	11.6%
Senior enlisted (E-7 and above)	63.1%	19.1%	3.8%	1.3%	1.2%	11.5%	14.3%
Enlisted (all)	67.4%	18.5%	4.3%	1.3%	1.3%	7.3%	17.5%
Total active duty	69.1%	16.8%	4.4%	1.2%	1.1%	7.5%	15.8%
U.S. resident population (ages 18–64)	76.2%	13.7%	6.3%	1.2%	0.3%	2.2%	17.9%

SOURCES: Kamarck, 2019, p. 21. Officer and enlisted figures are as reported by the Defense Manpower Data Center, May 2018. Annual Estimates of the Resident Population by Sex, Age, Race and Hispanic Origin for the United States, States, and Counties: April 1, 2010, to July 1, 2017, U.S. Census Bureau, Population Division, Release Date: July 1, 2017.

NOTE: Race and Hispanic origin are self-identified.

[a] The concept of race is separate from the concept of Hispanic origin. Hispanic may be more than one race (e.g., Hispanic and White or Hispanic and Black). Percentages for race should not be combined with the Hispanic percentage.

DBDI report, which used the "eligible population" language. We also note here that the concept of a merit-based system or meritocracy does not have a consistent definition. Although some sources may reference such a system as a DoD goal, it may mean different things in different contexts. In Chapter Four, we discuss the concept of merit in greater detail.

Lim, Cho, and Curry Hall, 2008, looks at diversity among Air Force officers and finds that minorities and women are underrepresented in the active-duty line officer population, particularly at the senior levels. The authors found that the disparities could primarily be explained by a difference in the candidate pool who were eligible for commission, which led to downstream disparities in more-senior ranks. In addition to this finding (as a contributing rather than competing explanation), Black and Hispanic promotion candidates were less likely to receive high review scores compared with White candidates with similar characteristics. Additionally, minority candidates were less likely to have markers of early career success, such as merit awards. This highlights the complexity of observed inequities. Although it should be desirable for DoD to increase its diversity in senior ranks, the cause of the disparity may stem from a combination of factors, such as representation earlier in the pipeline and potential bias in the performance review process. A 2020 RAND report presented similar findings among the White collar civilian workforce (Keller et al., 2020).

There also are concerns with regard to inequity in the military justice system, paralleling similar concerns in the wider criminal justice system. A report on disciplinary outcomes for Black individuals found disparities in the rates of disciplinary actions, investigations, and involuntary discharges as compared with White service members (Department of the Air Force Inspector General, 2020). The report also found disparities outside the justice system: notably, differences in career field placement, career advancement opportunities, and promotions.

Kriner and Shen, 2016, raises the issue of inequality in military casualties and wounded service members. The authors find that combat casualties are more likely to occur for individuals from lower socioeconomic communities, which they attribute to unequal selection into the military and into certain jobs from individuals of different socioeconomic backgrounds. They also examine inequality among support structures for veterans returning to different communities and whether decisions concerning warfare should take into account the unequal burden carried by different socioeconomic communities. We found no stated goals in DoD policies to address either inequality in military causalities or veteran outcomes.

In summary, much of this previous work points to the wide variety of problems that stem from inequity. Sometimes the causes of observed inequalities are complex and involve systemic structures that go beyond any one organization. According to the findings of these reports, many of the inequalities identified do not have any easy fix, or the disparities are caused by practices that comply with current laws and policies but lead to undesirable outcomes because of other, underlying structures. In this report, we do not seek to answer the broader questions of why inequalities exist or whether they are equitable or inequitable, but answering those questions is key to designing policy goals that guide the use of ML in decisionmaking processes.

As mentioned before, we focus only on process strategies specifically as they relate to decision points informed by algorithms. Prior research has shown the existence of racial inequalities in such areas as officer representation, promotion, and military justice. In many cases, the studies found structural reasons for the disparities. Some of these reasons are outside DoD's control, and some could be addressed through policy solutions. The remainder of this report addresses the question of what to do if the chosen policy solution concerns mitigating bias in a specific decision process, such as assignment or promotion. There are different ways of potentially mitigating bias, but we focus on the use of algorithms as an aid to human decisionmaking. The following chapter lays out this framework and considerations in order to ensure an equitable use of ML.

CHAPTER THREE

Machine Learning as an Aid to Decisionmaking

There is a growing interest in developing ML as a tool to aid decisionmaking in various settings across DoD. This reflects a recognition that these tools can make use of the significant amount of data collected and follows the direction that industry and other research fields are moving in terms of developing these new technologies. Automating parts of decisionmaking is an attractive proposition because automation imposes a level of consistency and possibly higher accuracy on the decisionmaking process. The availability of carefully curated data within the DoD ecosystem makes ML automation both attractive and often feasible, as some studies highlight (Schulker, Lim, et al., 2021).

In this report, we focus on ML applications that affect personnel management decisions within DoD. Other areas of ML development involve algorithms used for purely evaluative purposes rather than as direct inputs into decisionmaking (e.g., Morral et al., 2018) or applications that assist in decisionmaking processes that do not directly involve humans (e.g., Hartnett et al., 2020), but these areas are not the focus of our work. Later in this chapter, we provide further examples of the types of ML applications that are relevant to our work and are being developed by RAND researchers for DoD.

The application of automated decisionmaking (of any kind) to human subjects can incur normative concerns that extend beyond standard concerns of model verification and validation. Experiences in the private sector highlight some of these concerns (e.g., Dastin, 2018). To better understand the potential benefits and concerns, it is useful to have a structured view of ML-aided decisionmaking and adaptations to personnel-focused decisionmaking.

A Structured View of Algorithm-Aided Decisionmaking

Because ML algorithms are used in a broad variety of settings, we briefly detail the particular ML deployment context that we focus on throughout this report before reviewing relevant ML applications in the following section. Figure 3.1 outlines what we refer to as the *algorithm-aided decisionmaking framework*. This framework represents the process by which ML algorithms are developed and used in a decisionmaking context. The basic steps are as follows:

1. The ML algorithm is trained on historical data.
2. The algorithm is used to make predictions about the outcomes of new individuals.
3. Predictions are used as an input to a decisionmaking process made by a human.

For example, an algorithm used in a promotion selection setting may be trained to predict promotion selection decisions using a historical data set of performance reviews (Schulker, Lim, et al., 2021). A successfully trained algorithm would assign high scores to reviews of individuals who were promoted and low scores to reviews of individuals who were not promoted. Once trained, the algorithm can be used to score new performance reviews, and these scores can be provided as recommendations to influence new promotion selection decisions.

There are several potential benefits for incorporating ML algorithms into decisionmaking processes. One conceptual advantage of incorporating ML into decisionmaking is the ability to more clearly define the inputs and processes of the algorithm and maintain consistency across decisions. Additional benefits for incorporating ML come from improving efficiency through automation, potentially reducing the amount of human processing of large amounts of information. Another underlying motivation for the use of ML as an aid to decisionmaking is an understanding that the human processes are imperfect and do not always deliver equitable results. The hope is that algorithms that are properly implemented and audited lead to a more transparent and more equitable process.

Although there are advantages, there also are several barriers to attaining equity through algorithms. Although algorithms are often perceived as objective, it is vital to understand that algorithms can be biased. First, relying on historical data is potentially problematic. If the historical data set used to train the algorithm exhibits biases, there is a risk that those biases will be repeated by the algorithms' predictions. Relatedly, if the data do not sufficiently represent racial or ethnic minorities because they form a small number of historical cases, the resulting trained algorithm may have systematically poorer predictive performance within those underrepresented subgroups. Additionally, the implicit goals of an ML algorithm may conflict with equity. Although the goal of algorithmic training is often assumed to be maximizing overall predictive accuracy, equitable performance properties are not typically guaranteed by standard ML training objectives. In fact, the high overall predictive accuracy accomplished by typical ML training routines can be in direct competition with equity goals. In Chapter Four, we go into greater detail on this point.

Some of the methods discussed later in this report can help to address these issues. In general, however, if we use algorithms trained on historical data, we need to be aware of the validity of the historical data. Prior research, such as that discussed in Chapter Two, can help to understand whether historical biases may be present in available data. If known historical biases exist, extra precaution should be taken to avoid perpetuating such bias. We do not see the use of historical data as an insurmountable problem but one that should be realistically considered. We note that although current DoD processes for personnel decisions do not use ML, there is an increasing interest in using ML, as shown by the examples discussed in the following section.

In addition to the difficulties of attaining equity through algorithm-aided decision-making, a related important issue is that of transparency. Many standard ML algorithms may not be transparent, in the sense that the relationship between their data inputs and predictive outputs are difficult to understand. We do not discuss the transparency or interpretability of algorithms in this report, but we recommend Arrieta et al., 2020, and Lipton, 2018, on those topics as important corollaries to this report.

The process by which algorithmic output actually influences decisions varies by application. In the cases of résumé filtering for job applications or fully autonomous weaponry, algorithmic output may entirely determine an outcome. In the promotion selection example described earlier, algorithmic output may serve as one piece of evidence that is weighed alongside many others by a human decisionmaker. This report focuses on the equity properties of the ML component of the algorithmic decision framework, enclosed by the red box in Figure 3.1. In this report, we provide tools to audit the equity properties of algorithms, constrain algorithms to perform equitably, and weigh the inherent performance trade-offs. Algorithms might not replace human decisionmakers entirely but rather function as aids in the process. ML algorithms have the potential to leverage more information than would be possible by humans; if the underlying data and model are well understood, such algorithms should produce a transparent and auditable process.

Another potential pitfall is that when algorithmic tools are used as input for human decisions, the decisionmaker may choose to ignore the recommendation provided by the algo-

FIGURE 3.1
Algorithm-Aided Decision Framework

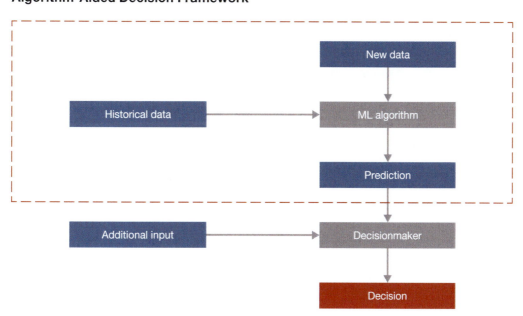

NOTE: In this report, we are primarily concerned with approaches to making the algorithmic component (enclosed by the dotted red line) of the decision process equitable.

rithm, as was shown in a recent implementation in Allegheny County (Chouldechova et al., 2018). Human decisionmaking processes that are downstream of the algorithmic component are not the focus of this report. However, these downstream processes are critical to overall equity of the decisionmaking process; an algorithm may produce equitable output that is ignored by an unfair human decisionmaker.

In this report, we focus on developing tools to identify and mitigate inequities introduced in the algorithmic portion of the decisionmaking process. If bias is introduced through other parts of the process, the methods discussed in this report will not guarantee that such bias is mitigated. We do not propose that our framework addresses equity in all ways or that equity can be described completely as a feature of the algorithm. The mitigating tools that we provide to enforce equitable outcomes cannot be used outside the predictive algorithmic context. Despite these limitations, the proposed framework may be useful in situations in which an algorithmic component is being considered to augment an existing decisionmaking framework that has desirable equity characteristics. The goal, in this scenario, is to ensure that the proposed introduction of an algorithmic component does not introduce new inequities. For instance, prior research suggests that the Air Force promotes service members at similar rates regardless of protected attributes once relevant characteristics are controlled for (Lim et al., 2014). If an algorithm were to be introduced into an existing process that was considered fair according to a particular definition of equity and the given policy directives, it should be audited to ensure it does not bias the process.

Examples of the Algorithm-Aided Decision Process for DoD

To conclude this chapter, we describe the primary areas of research into using ML to inform DoD decisions. We discuss applications that are currently deployed as well as applications for which there is ongoing investment and development. A review of non–personnel management research that focuses on the integration of ML into national security, including a review of all RAND publications developed from 2017 to 2021, is provided in Appendix C. For broader assessments of the breadth of ML applications in the military and in other areas of interest in DoD, see Tarraf et al., 2019, and Morgan et al., 2020. In this section, we highlight the applications in personnel management that are relevant to equity concerns.

DoD has started investing significantly in researching ML algorithms for personnel management. Both the Army and the Air Force are developing models and strategies for talent management. In one recent example, the Army requested proposals for software and/or strategies to help it recruit and distribute talent across the force, seeking "data science or machine learning solutions that will drastically change how it recruits, develops and distributes talent across the force" (GCN, 2020).

Prior RAND work has also produced numerous efforts on this topic. Schulker, Lim, et al., 2021, proposes an ML application to develop a performance-scoring system to manage talent in the Air Force. Also for the Air Force, Schulker, Harrington, et al., 2021, presents an early warning retention system to alert stakeholders of significant negative shifts in retention trends. The idea is to develop policies ahead of personnel shortages, once the model signals such a shift.

The Army is also reported to be developing a similar model (Heckman, 2020). The Army is also pursuing ML solutions in the security contracting process. The office of the Defense Security Service started a pilot program to apply an ML algorithm on people holding and seeking security clearances in order to predict employees who have betrayed or are at risk of betraying trust (Tucker, 2019).

In other, more general personnel management applications, Tong et al., 2020, builds on RAND's Dynamic Retention Model to predict retention and identify possible shortages. Similarly, Terry et al., 2019, presents a linear programming approach to project future officer inventory. Walsh et al., 2021, presents the Air Force Personnel Policy Assessment Application to simulate the effects of personnel policies on such factors as career field health and demographic diversity.

CHAPTER FOUR

Approaches to Auditing Machine Learning or Constraining It to Be Fair

The previous chapters demonstrate that DoD has both a commitment to DE&I and an interest in pursuing ML applications as an aid to decisionmaking. There is therefore a natural concern that ML applications developed by DoD may be at odds with its DE&I interests through algorithmic bias. In this chapter, we summarize some of the major concepts and findings from the algorithmic fairness literature to motivate our proposed framework and tool for developing equitable ML applications, described in Chapters Five and Six.

Two complementary aspects of ML are (1) auditing the equity characteristics of an algorithm and (2) constraining an algorithm to perform equitably. Auditing an ML algorithm involves assessing whether it has different performance properties across levels of a protected characteristic (e.g., different races and ethnicities). As will be discussed later in more detail, there are many ways to define algorithmic equity, each corresponding to different performance properties (e.g., balance of false positive versus balance of false negative rates across race and ethnicity). Constraining an algorithm to perform equitably involves altering the algorithm to reduce observed differences across a protected characteristic.

We emphasize that the types of inequities that we can audit and address correspond to predefined (and often narrow) definitions of algorithmic equity, which may not directly map onto all broader concepts of equity. Even when equity concepts are narrowly defined, an additional problem that we will discuss is that it is often impossible for algorithms to simultaneously satisfy multiple concepts of algorithmic equity. Further, identifying and addressing algorithmic inequities is particularly difficult when the existing process that generates the algorithmic training data exhibits biases, making it difficult to benchmark the predictions of the algorithm using the outcomes observed in the training data.

We emphasize that there is no universal approach to either auditing or enforcing equity. Equity audits are complicated by the fact that there are many equity definitions, each corresponding to different notions of fairness. Thus, an algorithm that performs equitably according to one definition may perform inequitably with respect to another. In each application, policy goals and legal mandates will help identify an appropriate equity definition. Another challenge is that constraining an algorithm to behave equitably typically comes at a cost to other performance properties. For example, enforcing equity may result in decreased predictive accuracy, which may lead to other negative consequences for decisionmakers.

In the remainder of this chapter, we review the available approaches for enforcing fairness in algorithms, connect select technical definitions of equity to specific DoD policy goals, and discuss the trade-offs inherent to enforcing fairness.

Binary Classification Setup

For simplicity, we consider binary classification algorithms throughout this report. Binary classification algorithms may be used to influence binary decisions, such as the decision to promote or not promote an individual. We refer to binary predictions as positive or negative, with positive corresponding to the assumed beneficial outcome, such as promotion. Predictions made from the algorithm typically are probabilities, which are then transformed to binary values based on a cutoff threshold. For example, a binary classification algorithm may predict promotion for a particular individual if the predicted probability of promotion is greater than 0.5 (or some other cutoff value). We note that, particularly in the algorithmic-assisted framework in which a human makes the final decision, the nonbinarized probabilities may be of more interest than the binarized predictions, since they carry more information. However, we note that prior work (such as Chouldechova et al., 2018, and Zhang, Liao, and Bellamy, 2020) shows that human decisionmakers may find working with nonbinary information difficult or may respond to it in nonlinear ways. In other words, they may not effectively use continuous information.

Most of the implemented methods available in the current iteration of the RAND Algorithmic Equity Tool directly modify the binarized predictions rather than the probabilities, primarily for ease of implementation and simplicity of presentation. (The pre-processing methods, discussed later, modify the input data only, allowing the user access to nonbinarized probabilities.) Future work may focus on methods for implementing equity interventions directly on continuous variables, but such interventions would require different methods for ensuring algorithmic fairness.

Classification algorithms are trained on historical data for which the true outcome is observed. The performance properties of an algorithm are derived by comparing algorithm predictions for historical data to historical outcomes. In the case of binary classification, there are four possible outcomes for each prediction: *true positive, false positive, true negative,* and *false negative.* These possibilities are summarized in Figure 4.1, which is commonly referred to as the *confusion matrix.* False positives and false negatives correspond to prediction errors: The algorithmic prediction and true outcome are not the same. For instance, an individual who was promoted but was not predicted to be promoted is a *false negative.* Conversely, an individual who was not promoted but was predicted to be promoted is a *false positive.*

Algorithmic performance can be described by various error rates. For instance, the *false positive rate* refers to the proportion of incorrect predictions made within the population of truly negative individuals. Likewise, the *false negative rate* refers to the proportion of incorrect

FIGURE 4.1

Confusion Matrix for the Binary Classification Problem

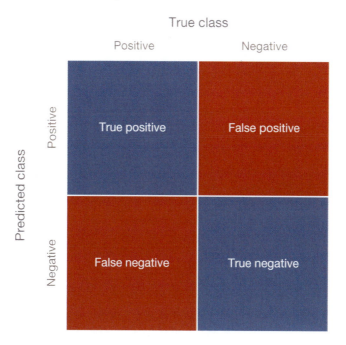

NOTE: Red cells indicate incorrect predictions, and blue cells indicate correct predictions.

predictions made within the population of truly positive individuals. The *overall error rate* of an algorithm refers to the proportion of incorrect predictions made in the entire population.

It is important to recognize that using false positive or false negative rates as performance metrics is only useful insofar as observed outcomes are a reasonable "gold standard" to compare predictions against. In the case of the promotional prediction example, if there is reason to believe that actual promotional decisions were poor historically, then it may be useful to develop alternative measures of achievement. For example, the outcome used in algorithmic training might be a measure that identifies those who should have been promoted based on other measures of career performance rather than historical promotional decisions. As noted in Chapter Three, prior literature on the possible biases in the historical data should be consulted prior to using the historical data as training data.

Algorithmic Equity Definitions

Algorithmic equity definitions concern properties of algorithmic predictions with respect to a *protected characteristic* (e.g., race), which has several *levels* (e.g., Black, White, and Hispanic). There are many different ways to define equity, and we will provide a very brief overview of several of the most important ones in this section. A more extensive and more rigorous review can be found in Appendix A.

Perhaps the simplest equity definition is *fairness through unawareness*. This definition simply requires that protected characteristics be removed from any input data upstream of algorithmic training. With respect to race, fairness through unawareness intuitively captures the notion of a "race-blind" decision. Despite its simplicity, many have noted that fairness through unawareness is a problematic notion within the ML framework. This is because simply removing protected characteristics may not actually remove their influence from predictions. For example, even if race is removed from the input data, an individual's race may be predicted with high confidence from other variables that remain in the data, such as geography. Even if race is removed, geography may act as a proxy for race.

Another simple equity definition is that of *statistical parity*. This definition requires that positive predictions occur at equal rates for each level of the protected class. When statistical parity holds, the demographics of the population that are predicted to belong to the positive class match the demographics of the entire population. Many additional equity concepts are constructed by comparing different error rates across levels of a protected characteristic. For example, an important equity definition is that of *false negative rate balance* (false negative rate balance is equivalent to *true positive rate balance*). For the case of promotions, false negative rate balance may require that the algorithm does not erroneously predict nonpromotion for one race at a higher rate than another. *False positive rate balance* is defined analogously (false positive rate balance is equivalent to *true negative rate balance*). *Equalized odds* is attained when both false positive rate balance and false negative rate balance are attained by an algorithm.

Approaches to Enforcing Algorithmic Equity

The fairness literature has developed many methods to enforce fairness. These methods differ both in the fairness criteria they enforce and in the stage of the algorithm at which the method intervenes. Methodologies typically are categorized into three classes: pre-processing, in-processing, and post-processing (Berk et al., 2021). *Pre-processing* refers to any method that alters the input data before they are used by the algorithm to produce predictions. *In-processing* refers to any corrective measure that intervenes during the ML training process. Finally, *post-processing* methods are applied entirely downstream of training the ML algorithm, directly adjusting the algorithmic predictions themselves. We connect the ideas of pre-processing and post-processing to the aforementioned concepts of procedural and outcome equity. Loosely speaking, we can view pre-processing methods as seeking to create procedural equity, whereas post-processing approaches are focused on producing outcome equity. We find these connections to be useful analogies, although they are not identical. Importantly, some pre-processing methods can have theoretical guarantees in terms of the distribution of outcomes (Johndrow and Lum, 2019).

Figure 4.2 summarizes the distinction between these methods. The RAND Algorithmic Equity Tool implements both pre-processing and post-processing methods but not in-processing methods. This is because pre-processing and post-processing methods are implemented independently from the development of the predictive ML algorithm and are therefore easier to apply in general. By contrast, in-processing methods require more-customized implementation. We provide further details of the pre- and post-processing methods implemented in the RAND Algorithmic Equity Tool below. A more thorough exploration of these ideas can be found in Berk et al., 2021.

Pre-Processing

Pre-processing methods typically seek transformations of the input training data that remove information about a protected characteristic. There are several attractive properties of pre-processing. First, it can be coupled with any predictive model, making it generally versatile. Second, it does not require the differential manipulation of output model predictions that depend explicitly on the protected characteristic, as is often the case for post-processing. For example, many post-processing methods require race-specific adjustments to predictions. When predictions are modified in a race-specific manner, there is a risk that the algorithm will be perceived as explicitly discriminatory. By contrast, pre-processing can be performed completely blind to the outcome of interest.

Removing the protected characteristic from the input data is the simplest form of pre-processing. Fairness through unawareness is therefore attained by the simple pre-processing procedure of redaction. Johndrow and Lum, 2019, provides a method for pre-processing that goes a step further than fairness through unawareness. Their method aims to transform input data, such that all variables are independent of the protected characteristic, while maintaining as much information as possible about the original distribution of input variables. They show that this method of pre-processing implicitly enforces statistical parity.

The RAND Algorithmic Equity Tool provides a simplified implementation of the Johndrow and Lum algorithm. Although the Johndrow and Lum algorithm insures mutual independence between all input data and the protected characteristic, our implementation only insures pairwise independence between the protected characteristic and each variable. We do not currently implement the full algorithm in the RAND Algorithmic Equity Tool because

FIGURE 4.2
Methods for Enforcing Equity Constraints

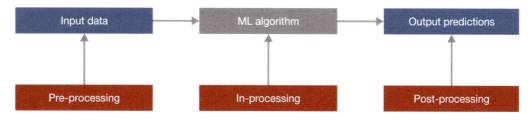

it is difficult to operationalize for general data sets that contain predictors with varying data types, but future implementations could consider an extended implementation.

In the algorithm-aided decisionmaking framework, pre-processing begins by altering the input data upstream of ML training. After the algorithm is trained on pre-processed data, both the predictive algorithm and the data transformations are passed to decisionmakers, who make predictions about new individuals. Data from the new individual must undergo the same transformation as the pre-processing data upstream of prediction. In the RAND Algorithmic Equity Tool, we recommend inputting both historical training data and the new data for which predictions will be made to the pre-processing algorithm. The RAND Algorithmic Equity Tool will automatically transform all data. The transformed historical data are then used to train the ML algorithm, and the transformed prediction data will be used to make new predictions.

Post-Processing

Post-processing methods are applied entirely downstream of ML training. As with pre-processing, post-processing is extremely versatile and can be paired with virtually any predictive model.

There is a broad literature on proposed post-processing methods. Damberg, Elliott, and Ewing, 2015, provides a simple post-processing method that adjusts model predictions to have equal means across levels of the protected characteristic. Although the method was introduced to enforce equity in pay-for-performance hospital reimbursement incentives, it is applicable more generally. Hardt, Price, and Srebro, 2016, proposes post-processing methods for enforcing false positive rate balance and false negative rate balance. Mishler, Kennedy, and Chouldechova, 2021, provides a post-processing method for enforcing counterfactual equalized odds: a form of fairness couched within a causal framework. The RAND Algorithmic Equity Tool implements a simple post-processing method that is capable of enforcing a wide array of equity definitions in a unified framework. As is common in most post-processing approaches, our method seeks optimal thresholds of positive prediction, which typically differ across levels of the protected characteristic. For example, a baseline algorithm may return a positive prediction for any individual with a predicted probability greater than 0.5. After post-processing, the algorithm may have a different threshold for positive prediction for each racial group. Further details of our post-processing method are described in Appendix B.

Mechanistically, post-processing is performed after ML training, and group-specific thresholds are returned. New predictions (not based on training data) are made using group-specific thresholds, and these binary predictions are returned to decisionmakers. If the new data and historical data are drawn from similar populations, then the new binary predictions should attain equity priorities.

The human component of the algorithm-assisted decisionmaking process, in which a human receives and interprets the algorithmic prediction before making a final decision, can also be thought of as a form of post-processing. Like the post-processing methods described here, human post-processing can have a significant effect on the final distribution of outcomes. The primary distinction between human post-processing and algorithmic post-processing is that algorithmic post-processing can be used to attain specific equity goals in a well-defined manner using a complex set of inputs, whereas the post-processing performed by a human, though potentially rule-based, may be ad hoc and inconsistently applied. For example, promotion boards might be provided information about the race and ethnicity of candidates and told that diversity is an important value in their decisions, without specific guidance concerning how to implement that value.

Inherent Trade-Offs to Enforcing Equity

When enforcing any particular equity priority, it is important to understand that there are significant inherent trade-offs. These include

1. conflicts between equity priorities
2. conflicts between equity priorities and performance priorities
3. conflicts between equity and legal mandates.

The first important trade-off is that different equity concepts typically conflict with one another. As a simple example, it is generally not possible to satisfy statistical parity and false negative rate balance simultaneously. In the example of promotion selection predictions, this means that you can develop an algorithm that either (1) ensures that each racial group is predicted to be promoted at the same rate or (2) ensures that erroneous negative predictions do not happen more for one racial group than another. Unfortunately, it is usually not possible to develop an algorithm that ensures that both of these equity priorities are met exactly. To see why, consider the following example. Suppose one racial group has historically been promoted at higher rates than another racial group. To make algorithmic predictions obey statistical parity, the algorithm will need to either make more incorrect negative (do not promote) predictions for individuals belonging to the historically overrepresented group or make more incorrect positive (do promote) predictions for individuals belonging to the underrepresented group. In either case, it would be impossible to also obtain equal false negative (or true positive) rates.

There is a large literature documenting the mutual incompatibility of various fairness definitions, which we review at the end of Appendix A. To briefly summarize these findings, however, it is usually impossible to exactly satisfy multiple equity definitions simultaneously. Consequently, all predictive algorithms will violate certain equity concepts. When designing an equitable algorithm, it is therefore necessary to be specific about the type of equity to enforce. We reiterate this point when providing our framework for developing equitable algorithms in Chapters Five and Six. It is important to note that these *impossibility theorems*, as they are often called, are not specific to algorithms. Regardless of the method by which decisions are made—whether algorithmic or human—satisfying multiple notions of equity is a fundamental challenge.

In addition to navigating conflicts between equity definitions, enforcing equity may come at the cost of other priorities. Typically, overall accuracy suffers when an algorithm is constrained to perform equitably. The trade-off between equity and accuracy can have real-world repercussions. For instance, Corbett-Davies et al., 2017, illustrates an inherent trade-off between public safety concerns and one set of equity concerns in an algorithm to predict violent recidivism. Demanding equitable performance characteristics according to their chosen definitions, they argued, would result in increased violent crime. Because of the possible competition between fairness and accuracy, especially when using historical data to measure accuracy, our tool allows developers to compare multiple equity interventions across multiple accuracy metrics in order to explicitly quantify this trade-off.

A final important consideration when implementing an equity intervention is that the intervention should satisfy policy mandates. For example, enforcing racial statistical parity in hiring decisions requires enforcing a type of racial quota, which often are explicitly prohibited. This is because statistical parity requires that a specific proportion (determined by demographic statistics) of promoted individuals come from each race or ethnicity group, which is equivalent to numerical quotas for each race or ethnicity. In the next section, we give examples of ways to connect technical equity definitions to DoD policy.

Connecting DoD Policies to Equity Definitions

In this section, we aim to identify connections between the formal equity concepts described earlier and DoD policies regarding personnel management. We emphasize that this is not an exact science, since policy directives are not written explicitly with technical equity norms in mind. However, connecting policy recommendations to specific equity definitions is necessary to appropriately audit ML algorithms. This exercise will be useful in the framework we provide in the next chapter for developing equitable ML algorithms.

We consider three ideals expressed as equity priorities by DoD: (1) decisions should be blind to protected characteristics, (2) merit should be rewarded, and (3) the demographics of DoD should reflect the nation it serves. Although we find these to be the most clearly stated ideals, we do not imply that these encompass the entirety of DoD's personnel policies. We also note that the connections between the policy goals and equity definitions contain some uncertainty because many of the policy directives are not written in language that perfectly translates to technical meanings. The following three connections are possible, not definitive, readings of DoD policy.

Policy Connection 1: Not Explicitly Considering Protected Characteristics—Fairness Through Unawareness

One priority found in DoD policies is that individuals should not be treated differently purely on account of protected characteristics, such as gender or race. Although there are some exceptions for certain restrictions on age or physical ability, a common DoD principle is that individuals who are alike except in terms of protected characteristics should be treated alike. This principle can be seen, for example, through directives that discourage the use of diversity quotas, such as the Air Force Instruction on diversity and inclusion or the National Defense Authorization Act for Fiscal Year 2013 (Air Force Instruction 36-7001, 2019; Pub. L. 112-239, 2013). It can also been seen in a recent move by the Secretary of Defense to consider removing photos and names from promotion selection packets in order to avoid explicitly considering an individual's race or gender (Dickstein, 2020).

We connect this concept to the equity definition of fairness through unawareness because the redaction of protected characteristics from these decisionmaking processes mirrors the exclusion of protected characteristics as input data to the algorithm, which is required to achieve fairness through unawareness. As noted earlier, simply redacting a protected characteristic is rarely sufficient to remove its influence. This is because protected characteristics may be strongly correlated with other factors used in prediction, which in turn may inappropriately act as proxies for the redacted factor. For example, graduation from a Historically Black College or University (HBCU) is strongly correlated with race. Redacting race but retaining graduation from an HBCU may not sufficiently remove the influence of race. We therefore also connect DoD's priority of ignoring protected characteristics with pre-processing methods that remove correlations between race and other factors used in prediction. These pre-processing procedures, which may be thought of as stronger forms of fairness through unawareness, arguably better capture DoD's priority of ignoring protected characteristics. We explore the utility of these pre-processing methods in Chapter Six.

Policy Connection 2: Building the Best Fighting Force and Merit-Based Achievements—True Positive Balance or False Negative Balance

DoD's policies express the ideal that all individuals should be rewarded based on merit. Underlying this is DoD's goal of developing the strongest and most capable personnel in order to achieve mission readiness and supremacy as a fighting force. DoD has argued that equity priorities complement the ideal of a meritocracy. As described in the 2012–2017 strategic initiative,

> Diversity is a strategic imperative, critical to mission readiness and accomplishment . . . we must focus our efforts on emerging diverse markets to successfully attract, recruit, and retain a highly-skilled workforce capable of meeting current and future readiness and mission requirements. (DoD, 2012, p. 3)

We connect the concept of meritocracy to the equity definition of true positive balance. Considering promotion as an example, true positive balance implies that individuals who merit promotion are promoted at equal rates across different levels of a protected characteristic (e.g., racial groups). We note that true positive balance is equivalent to false negative balance (since a change in the true positive rate indicates an equivalent corresponding change in the false negative rate). From this perspective, false negative balance ensures that individuals who merit promotion are not discriminatorily denied promotion on the basis of their race.

We note that we informally use the word *merit* in the descriptions above to intuitively convey the notion of true positive balance. In the actual ML context, true positive balance requires that individuals who are actually promoted are correctly predicted to be promoted at equal rates across levels of the protected characteristic. Whether the population of promoted individuals observed in the historical data do indeed merit promotion assumes that the historical promotion process is an accurate measure of merit. In other words, true positive rate balance is only a valid interpretation of meritocracy if the historical promotions used to train the data are a desirable standard to emulate. If different standards were required historically for promotion for different levels of the protected characteristic, then true positive rate balance would not be appropriate. For example, it may be true that less deserving individuals from one group received promotion at higher rates, while individuals from another group had to work harder to receive promotions. If the historical promotion selection process is biased in the sense that individuals from one population face higher barriers to promotion than individuals from another population, then it would not reflect a meritocratic procedure; promoted individuals from the advantaged class would exhibit less merit. As noted in Chapter Three, we recommend reviewing the prior work to assess the validity of historical data before using algorithms trained on such data. For example, there is some evidence to suggest that historical promotional decisions are not explicitly non-meritocratic. For instance, Lim et al., 2014, argues that Air Force officer promotion decisions do not differ across race or gender for individuals with similar records, which would suggest the historical process was equitable according to a particular definition of fairness.

True positive rate balance is also desirable because predictive algorithms may have differential predictive accuracy for different groups, for reasons such as historical bias, majority influence, nonrepresentative data, or predictors that are not equally predictive for each group. The last possibility was recognized in the 2020 DBDI report, which recommended a review of the military aptitude tests to analyze whether they "adversely impact diversity and are unrelated to predictive validity" (DBDI, 2020, p. ix).

Although true positive balance (or false negative balance) provides a natural connection to the idea of meritocracy, this is certainly not the only related equity definition. Indeed, the notion of *meritocracy* is sufficiently broad as to allow for connections between it and many equity concepts. For instance, one can similarly connect false positive (or, equivalently, true negative) balance to meritocracy. Returning to the promotion selection example, false positive balance suggests that truly unqualified individuals are not erroneously predicted as promoted at different rates across levels of the protected class. Just as it is difficult to call a process meritocratic if it differentially rewards truly deserving individuals, it is also difficult to call a process meritocratic if it differentially rewards truly undeserving individuals. One can similarly make connections between the idea of meritocracy and the equity definitions of positive predictive balance and negative predicted balance (described in detail in Appendix A). It also is possible to connect fairness through unawareness to meritocracy: A meritocracy should only consider measures of merit and be blind to all other individual-level attributes.

As mentioned previously in this section, multiple formal equity concepts are often not simultaneously attainable. The multitude of equity concepts that are related to the notion of meritocracy therefore poses a significant challenge to enforcing equity. Ultimately, the decision for how to define merit and connect it to a definition of algorithmic equity will lie in the hands of informed policymakers. The connection we make here to true positive rate balance represents our best understanding of the policies as currently written. If DoD further clarified the term *merit*, in terms of how it is defined, measured, and rewarded, then more-precise connections to algorithmic fairness would be possible.

Policy Connection 3: Demographic Representation of the U.S. Eligible Population—Statistical Parity

Lastly, DoD consistently expresses a desire that its workforce reflect the eligible U.S. population. This concept may be the most frequently referenced ideal. For example, the 2020 DBDI report's Recommendation 1.2 is to "achieve a talent pipeline reflecting the diversity of the current and future eligible population from U.S. Census projections" (DBDI, 2020, p. ix), and the measure of success will be when data can "show that racial and ethnic representation within the military is more consistent across all grades and the number of minorities to be retained beyond initial commitment and promoted to senior grades increases" (DBDI, 2020, p. 22). We connect this concept to the equity definition of *statistical parity*, which means that individuals of different races receive positive outcomes at an equal rate.

Returning to the promotion selection example, statistical parity implies that an equal proportion of candidates from different racial groups receive promotion. We note that in relation to DoD policies stated earlier, statistical parity only provides representation at the higher grade levels if there is adequate representation at the lower levels. If disparities exist at earlier stages of promotion selection, promoting individuals at equal rates will only maintain the same representation. In other words, to connect to DoD's policy goals, statistical parity would need to work in tandem with a talent pipeline that started with a pool of applicants that reflects the eligible population. We know this is not currently the case. As shown in Table 2.1, for example, some racial and ethnic groups are already underrepresented at earlier stages for officers.

Rather than enforcing statistical parity with respect to the applicant pool, an alternative is to directly require that the demographic composition of the population who receive positive predictions matches a specific target distribution, such as the racial demographics of the entire United States or some eligible subset of that population. This would result in overselecting the underrepresented group within the applicant pool (rather than selecting at equal rates across all groups, as would be the case in standard statistical parity). We acknowledge that this is a viable alternative, but we will consider standard statistical parity throughout this work. Although DoD policies express a desire to reflect the nation DoD serves, there is tension with the idea of overselecting certain groups to achieve that representation (such as restricting quotas).

Alternative concepts of non-exact statistical parity might be more amenable to DoD under its current policies. The concept of parity has been connected to the legal concept of disparate impact, which concerns whether certain processes lead to disparate outcomes for groups with different protected characteristics. The Civilian Equal Employment Opportunity and Military Equal Opportunity programs do not contain specific definitions of disparate impact, but the EEOC has long advocated the use of a "four-fifths rule" to identify disparate impact (U.S. Equal Employment Opportunity Commission, 1979). According to the four-fifths rule, the selection rate of the least-selected group is not less than 80 percent of the selection rate of the most-selected group. The four-fifths rule is another mathematically well-defined notion of parity that serves as a reasonable alternative to the standard statistical parity considered in this report. Under this framework, DoD might move toward closer representation without requiring exact quotas.

CHAPTER FIVE

A Framework for Developing Equitable Machine Learning Algorithms

In this chapter, we present the RAND Algorithmic Equity Tool and discuss the general rationale and considerations for each step. In the next chapter, we demonstrate the tool's use with a hypothetical ML application drawn from the personnel management space. The five steps are as follows:

1. determine equity risk
2. identify relevant equity mandates and priorities
3. determine relevant equity definitions
4. identify important overall performance priorities
5. weigh trade-offs of enforcing equity.

Determine Equity Risk

An important initial step is to determine whether the ML algorithm in question poses an equity risk. Whether an algorithm poses an equity risk is determined by the context in which the algorithm is deployed. Although it may be difficult to anticipate the downstream equity impact of any particular ML algorithm, the following two factors generally heighten the equity risk:

1. The algorithm output directly influences a decision.
2. Those decisions directly affect individual people.

Although these two factors are not the only ones that can signal an equity risk, most high-profile cases concerning algorithmic equity share these characteristics. The following are some examples:

- The well-studied Correctional Offender Management Profiling for Alternative Sanctions (COMPAS) algorithm produced recidivism risk scores for defendants that were then considered by judges during sentencing procedures (Angwin et al., 2016). Individual-level predictive recidivism scores were used to influence individual bail and sentencing decisions. The algorithm was criticized because it incorrectly predicted recidivism among Black defendants at a higher rate than it did for White defendants.

- Amazon developed an algorithm that generated automated scores based on candidate résumés (Dastin, 2018). These résumé scores were reviewed by Amazon's recruiters (although it is unclear to what degree these scores were actually used in hiring decisions). The project was disbanded because of concerns that the algorithm learned to systematically penalize applications that identifiably belonged to women. For example, inclusion of the word "women" within the text of a résumé (e.g., "women's rugby team") incurred a penalty.

- Many hospitals rely on algorithms to identify patients of various risk categorizations. These risk scores are used to recommend individual patients to "high-risk care management" programs, which provide additional resources. There has been concern that these algorithms systematically give lower risk scores to Black patients compared to White patients with similar medical conditions (Obermeyer et al., 2019).

In addition to the two primary factors highlighted in this section, another important consideration is whether already disadvantaged groups are likely to be negatively affected by the introduction of a proposed ML algorithm into a decisionmaking process. Depending on the setting, this circumstance may be more concerning from an equity perspective than if members of advantaged groups face potentially adverse or equalizing effects. If an ML application does not pose a direct equity risk, it is likely unnecessary to evaluate its equity properties.

Identify Relevant Equity Mandates and Priorities

After identifying whether a given ML application poses an equity risk, the next step is to understand the legal requirements and institutional priorities regarding equity that are relevant to the domain in which the algorithm is applied. For example, Amazon's résumé-scoring algorithm may not have been in compliance with Equal Employment Opportunity (Title VII of the Civil Rights Act of 1964), which protects against workplace discrimination on the basis of many protected characteristics, including sex (Goodman, 2018). Importantly, Equal Employment Opportunity protects against both disparate treatment and disparate impact. Whereas disparate treatment is generally interpreted as "intentional" discrimination, disparate impact protects against seemingly race-neutral policies that disproportionately affect protected groups. In addition to legal prohibitions against workplace discrimination, a résumé-scoring system that implicitly penalizes female candidates is counter to Amazon's statements regarding diversity in hiring (Amazon, undated). This application provides an example of why explainable models are vital in addition to the need for fairness.

Legal mandates regarding equity can have important differences across domains. For instance, the legal equity mandates regarding insurance pricing require that rates are not *unfairly discriminatory*. Importantly, unfair discrimination in this context does not preclude the possibility of average premiums differing across levels of a protected attribute, so long as those differences reflect differences in risk. Unlike Equal Employment Opportunity, insurance pricing does not directly limit the possibility of pricing policies with disparate impact. Osoba et al., 2019, provides an overview for identifying equity concepts in civilian domains that have encountered algorithmic equity concerns, including insurance industries, hiring practices, and criminal justice.

Determine Relevant Equity Definitions

After identifying the legal requirements and institutional priorities that are relevant to the decision environment, these must be translated to concrete, mathematical equity definitions. This can be a difficult task, since legal mandates and institutional priorities related to equity are seldom stated in terms that easily map onto technical definitions of fairness.

The EEOC four-fifths rule is a rare instance in which an equity concept is described with sufficient detail to unambiguously assign a mathematical criterion (Feldman et al., 2015). In particular, the four-fifths rule defines a form of approximate statistical parity, in which the selection rate of the least-selected group is not less than 80 percent that of the most-selected group (see Appendix A for further details). In most cases, however, mathematical translation is far less clear. So far, the Supreme Court has explicitly resisted providing concrete, mathematical formulations of equity definitions.

To assist in the difficult process of matching equity goals to mathematical definitions, others have provided helpful guidelines for general settings. The decision tree shown in Figure 5.1, which we simplified and adapted from Aequitas (Saleiro et al., 2018), is one such example. As an example of how to use this decision tree, consider the question of racial bias in the COMPAS recidivism risk score introduced earlier in this chapter. Beginning at the

FIGURE 5.1

Fairness Decision Tree Adapted from Aequitas

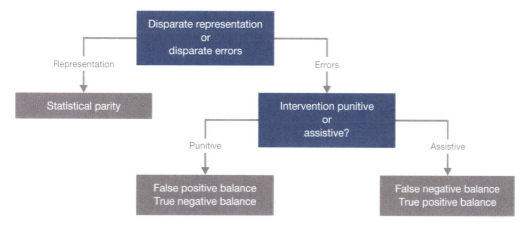

SOURCE: Adapted from Saleiro et al., 2018, p. 9.

first node of the decision tree, one first decides whether equitable representation or equitable errors are sought. For the purposes of predicting recidivism, equal representation may not be an appropriate measure. If true recidivism rates vary by race, requiring an algorithm to predict equal recidivism rates may result in poor accuracy. However, for the algorithm to be useful in a legal or policing setting, it is desirable to require that an algorithm used to predict recidivism is equally accurate for different racial groups.[1] Following the decision tree, we would choose to move down the right branch ("Errors") and onto the second question. Because the algorithm is used in a punitive setting (e.g., positive predictions result in punitive outcomes), we would choose to move down the left branch ("Punitive"), and we find that balancing false positive rates (or, equivalently, true negative rates) is an appropriate mathematical equity goal. Achieving false positive rate balance would ensure that, among those who truly did not recidivate, errors occur at the same rate for advantaged and disadvantaged groups. Intuitively, this avoids a circumstance in which innocent individuals from disadvantaged racial groups bear a disproportionate burden of inaccurate predictions. It is reasonable to argue that further harms to those who are already disadvantaged are more costly and that avoiding such harms should be prioritized.

Indeed, it was precisely the lack of false positive balance, first identified by Angwin et al., 2016, that initially drew criticism with respect to the COMPAS algorithm. We emphasize that this decision tree is meant to provide a reasonable rule of thumb. In general, translating equity priorities to mathematical definitions should be done on a case-by-case basis. There are many other cases and potential equity definitions, which can be seen in the full decision tree provided by Saleiro et al., 2018.

In Chapter Four, we identified connections between three common equity priorities concerning DoD personnel and formal equity definitions. As discussed in Chapter Four, it is possible that multiple fairness metrics conflict with one another. When identifying relevant equity definitions, it is therefore advisable to choose only the most important ones. In the event that multiple definitions are considered, the RAND Algorithmic Equity Tool gives the user the ability to compare multiple equity interventions across multiple fairness metrics.

Identify Important Overall Performance Priorities

Although equity attributes are important to monitor when an algorithm poses an equity risk, there typically are other important performance priorities not directly related to equity that should be assessed. Although equity is often characterized by an algorithm's comparative behavior across levels of a protected group, overall performance (i.e., without regard to protected characteristics) is typically also of interest. For example, in research on equity

---

[1] As previously noted, accuracy with respect to historical data is only useful insofar as outcomes in the historical data set are a reasonable standard to attain; this is arguably not the case for historical arrest data. This example is only meant to serve an illustrative purpose.

in lending, the disparity in proportions of loans acquired by individuals of different races has been balanced against the amount of total profit the lending company can expect to make (Hardt, Price, and Srebro, 2016). Monitoring overall performance priorities is essential because enforcing equity typically comes at a cost to overall performance. To understand this trade-off, note that any algorithm can perform equitably with respect to false positive balance, false negative balance, and statistical parity by simply outputting a positive prediction for all individuals, blind to all individual attributes (protected or otherwise). False positive balance is attained because, among individuals who are truly "negative," all are predicted as positives regardless of their protected attributes. Similarly, false negative balance is attained because, among individuals who are truly "positive," none are incorrectly misclassified. Finally, statistical parity is attained because all groups attain positive predictions at the same rate (100 percent). Although such an algorithm will have equitable performance with respect to these measures, the overall accuracy of the algorithm may be poor.

To appropriately weigh the trade-offs of enforcing equity (which is performed in the next step), it is important to first identify the overall performance priorities of interest. The most common overall performance priority is predictive accuracy, which measures the proportion of correct predictions by comparing algorithmic predictions to true outcomes observed in training data. Accuracy is typically connected to some desirable outcome, such as lending to individuals who will pay interest and not default, for which higher accuracy is associated with greater benefit to certain parties. In some situations, other performance priorities may be more important than overall predictive accuracy. For instance, if a facial recognition algorithm is used to identify dangerous individuals on a watch list, incorrectly predicting that individuals are not on the watch list (false negative) may be much more consequential than incorrectly predicting that they are (false positive). In this scenario, minimizing false negatives may be prioritized over minimizing false positives because of the security threats posed by a false negative.

Weigh Trade-Offs of Enforcing Equity

After identifying relevant equity norms and overall performance priorities, the final step is to apply appropriate equity interventions and assess the trade-offs of doing so. The RAND Algorithmic Equity Tool is primarily designed to assist in this final step.

The RAND Algorithmic Equity Tool allows users to pre-process input data or post-process algorithmic predictions using a suite of methodologies described in Chapter Four. Users can use the tool to assess the comparative equity and overall performance properties of each intervention. To evaluate the effect of pre-processing, the tool allows users to input algorithmic predictions derived from different sets of training data (e.g., the original data set versus the pre-processed data set). One can similarly use the tool to assess the equity performance of any set of candidate algorithms, which potentially differ in their model specification rather than their training data. To evaluate the effects of post-processing, the tool allows users to apply several different post-processing methods to predictions from a single algorithm.

As discussed previously, improvements from the perspective of one equity priority can come at the cost of negative consequences from the perspective of another. It is important that trade-offs in different types of equity are considered, not just trade-offs between equity and performance. This should involve dialogue with stakeholders and equity experts to determine the most important equity mandates and acceptable levels of trade-off between equity measures and overall performance. An important feature of the RAND Algorithmic Equity Tool is that it allows one to visualize the impact of algorithm modifications on both selected equity and overall performance priorities. We envision that this tool can be used during the developmental stages of an algorithm intended for use in an algorithm-assisted decisionmaking process. Doing so would necessitate careful and explicit thinking about equity priorities—potentially, facilitating early conversations between developers and stakeholders—before algorithmic deployment can inadvertently result in unacceptable biases. There are various frameworks for how to provide algorithmic output to human decisionmakers, and we do not explicitly explore questions such as how much weight should be given by humans to the algorithmic output. In the following chapter, we provide a detailed illustration of how the RAND Algorithmic Equity Tool can be leveraged, assuming that decisionmakers will be provided with binary recommendations.

CHAPTER SIX

Demonstration of Equity Framework Through a Hypothetical Case Study

In this chapter, we demonstrate the workflow described in the previous chapter for a hypothetical algorithm used to assist in DoD promotion decisions. We emphasize that the method evaluated in this chapter is intended only to provide an illustration of our developed tools and does not reflect any current DoD practice.

Hypothetical Case Study Description: Promotion Prediction

To illustrate, we consider a hypothetical ML application developed to predict promotion selection decisions on the basis of individual-level data. We imagine that this algorithm has been trained on historical data consisting of a large set of individual-level attributes paired with actual promotion selection decisions. Although the algorithm we evaluate is purely for illustrative purposes and trained on simulated data, we note that similar applications have been proposed. For instance, Schulker, Lim, et al., 2021, proposes an exploratory ML tool (not currently used by DoD) capable of predicting promotion selection decisions from evaluations provided in essay-style narrative performance reviews.

The output of this algorithm is a predicted probability of promotion for each individual. This predicted probability, which is a numerical value ranging from zero to one, may be used as a score at the time of the promotion selection decision. Higher predicted probabilities of promotion are viewed as indicative of an individual exhibiting attributes similar to those promoted in the past. The predicted probabilities may also be binarized by thresholding; individuals with high predicted probabilities are predicted to be promoted, and individuals with low predicted probabilities are predicted not to be promoted. These binary predictions may also be considered as binary classifications of applicant quality at the time of promotion decisions.

Determine Equity Risk

The equity risk of this predictive tool depends on the way the tool is used. For instance, Schulker, Lim, et al., 2021, provides several possible uses for the predictive tool, each of which has different equity risks. One potential use is to broadly inform personnel management policies. In this setting, the individual-level promotion probabilities generated by a predictive algorithm would be pooled together to provide an overall index of the performance properties of a particular subdivision of the larger force (e.g., Air Force pilots). A subdivision composed of many individuals with high predicted probabilities of promotion might be considered high-performing, and vice versa. If the algorithms predicted lower probabilities of promotion for minority service members relative to similarly qualified White service members, for instance, then subdivisions consisting of large proportions of minorities would have artificially lower aggregate quality estimates. Whether this poses an equity risk depends on what decisions are made in response to this aggregate quality measure. For instance, if low aggregate scores triggered changes to recruitment strategy by allocating additional recruitment resources to underperforming divisions, then the inequitable predictions may result in overall resource inefficiencies, but they are unlikely to negatively affect the minority service members whose quality was underestimated. If, on the other hand, a punitive measure was taken against subdivisions with perceived lagging performance according to this measure, then the inequitable predictions may indeed pose an equity risk. Although the algorithmic output is used to inform higher-level policy decisions, individual-level predictions are not used to guide individual-level decisions, generally mitigating the equity risk posed by this type of application.

Another way this algorithmic output could be used is to guide competitive promotion selection decisions. In this setting, the individual-level prediction output would be used as input to promotion decisions; high scores would be viewed favorably by managers at the time of promotion, while low scores would be viewed negatively. Here, individual-level decisions are affected by the individual-level predictions of an algorithm. Consequently, the equity risk posed by the algorithm in this setting is considerable. Inequitable performance properties of the algorithm may result in inequitable promotion selection decisions. For the purposes of illustration, we will assume that the promotion selection predictions will be used in this setting throughout the remainder of this chapter.

Identify Relevant Equity Mandates and Priorities

As we outlined in Chapter Four, DoD's equity priorities regarding personnel, as expressed through its written policies and statements, can be summarized by three overarching goals:

1. **Blinded.** Career entry and progression within DoD should be blind with respect to protected attributes.
2. **Meritocratic.** DoD should function meritocratically by recognizing and rewarding performance.
3. **Representative.** DoD should reflect the demographics of the country it serves.

As discussed previously, multiple equity goals will typically not be simultaneously attainable. Therefore, policymakers are encouraged to communicate with ML developers in order to prioritize equity goals. For the purposes of this illustration, however, we will monitor each of these goals and not prioritize any one of them.

Identifying Relevant Equity Definitions

To enforce these three DoD equity goals, they need to be translated into concrete mathematical language. In Chapter Four, we explored connections between these three equity goals and formal equity definitions. Although we note that this generally is a difficult task, we suggest the following three translations:

1. blinded → fairness through unawareness
2. meritocratic → false negative or true positive balance
3. representative → statistical parity.

These three translations are not meant to be definitive for all applications; careful consideration should be taken when translating informal policy language into formal mathematical equity priorities. Below, we describe some of the relevant assumptions and considerations that would be necessary to justify these translations.

Blinded → Fairness Through Unawareness

To justify fairness through unawareness as a valid strategy for blinding decisions to protected characteristics, one must assume that inappropriate proxies of protected characteristics do not remain in the training data after the protected characteristics have been retracted. The résumé scoring tool from Amazon provides such an example (Dastin, 2018). Although applicant sex was not a provided predictor, words revealing applicant sex (e.g., "women's rugby team") still existed in the text of applicant résumés and were shown to be penalized by the algorithm. When it is possible that inappropriate proxies remain after protected attributes are redacted, one should not rely on fairness through unawareness alone. A stronger form of pre-processing than fairness through unawareness, which removes all correlations between protected characteristics and predictor variables, is also considered in this example.

Meritocratic → False Negative or True Positive Rate Balance

In the context of a promotion prediction, true positive balance requires that truly promoted individuals are predicted to be promoted at the same rate regardless of their protected characteristics. This is only a valid mathematical interpretation of meritocracy if the historical promotions used to train the data are a desirable standard to emulate. If different standards were required for promotion for different levels of the protected characteristic, then true positive rate balance may not be appropriate. For instance, suppose that higher levels of merit were historically required to promote for members of a disadvantaged class. In that case, the population of truly promoted individuals from the disadvantaged class will be of higher merit than the population of truly promoted individuals from the advantaged class. Predicting promotions from both groups at the same rate, as would be done if true positive rate balance were attained, would not reflect a meritocratic procedure. This is because the historically promoted individuals from the advantaged class are less deserving.

Representative → Statistical Parity

The most straightforward translation is between representativeness and statistical parity. However, there is some ambiguity regarding exactly how statistical parity should be enforced. An important question to answer is whether, at each promotion selection stage, aggregate national demographics should be reflected or whether the demographics of the relevant eligible population should be reflected. For instance, Kamarck, 2019, notes that although the demographics of officers upon entry do not reflect the national demographics of the United States, they do reflect the demographics of the population of college-educated individuals. Because the demographics of college-educated people differ from the national demographics, initial officer selection occurring at equal rates across racial groups within the eligible population will result in a population of officers that does not reflect the national demographics. For the purposes of this illustration, we assume that the target population is the subpopulation that is eligible for promotion.

Identifying Important Non-Equity Performance Priorities

In addition to the equity priorities of a promotion selection prediction algorithm, there are important non-equity performance concerns. As with most ML applications, overall accuracy, measured as the proportion of correct predictions based on training data, is a natural priority. We will use this performance measure when weighing trade-offs in the following step.

Weighing Trade-Offs

After equity and non-equity performance priorities are identified, we can now intervene with the candidate ML algorithm and weigh the costs and benefits of doing so. We will present the results of pre- and post-processing methods here, which are available in our provided tool and described in further detail in Chapter Four. Although the underlying data used in these illustrations are simulated, they are useful to demonstrate typical trade-offs.

Pre-Processing Interventions

Using the provided tool, we can weigh the equity and performance trade-offs resulting from training the ML algorithm on three data sets. A baseline data set includes all available covariates in the prediction, including race. The second training data set is identical to the baseline data set, except that race is not included. This second training data set reflects fairness through unawareness. A final training data set is generated by modifying the baseline data set using a pre-processing method introduced by Johndrow and Lum, 2019. This method is discussed further in Chapter Four and is implemented in our provided tool.

Figure 6.1, which is output from the RAND Algorithmic Equity Tool, displays the equity characteristics of the predictive algorithm after training on each of these three data sets. As discussed above, an understanding of the equity priorities related to promotion selection decisions leads us to focus on statistical parity and false negative rate balance as appropriate equity metrics. As a measure of statistical parity, we compute the proportion of predicted promotions for each racial group. Note that equal rates of promotion across racial categories will result in a promoted population that has the same demographics as the population eligible for promotion.

The left panel of Figure 6.1 shows that promotions are predicted at higher rates for the advantaged racial group than for the disadvantaged racial group when the algorithm is

FIGURE 6.1

Equity Measures Compared Across Racial Categories for Each Pre-Processing Method

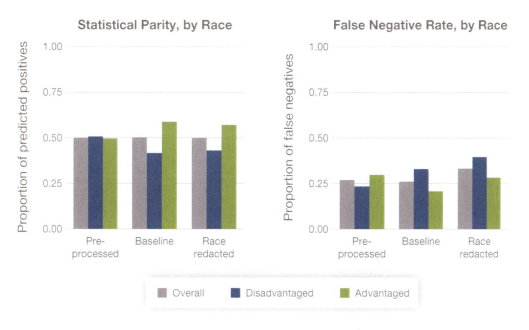

NOTE: The left panel shows a comparison of the proportion of positives predicted ($\hat{Y} = 1$) for each racial category, and the right panel shows a comparison of the false negative rates for each racial category.

trained on the baseline data or the race-redacted data. For the ML algorithm trained on the pre-processed data set, however, promotions are predicted at equal rates across race. Thus, statistical parity is attained by data pre-processing. With respect to true positive rates (or, equivalently, false negative rates), the right panel of Figure 6.1 shows that all methods display imbalance across racial groups. While achieving statistical parity, pre-processing affects other equity metrics. For example, although training on the baseline data sets results in higher false negative rates for the disadvantaged racial category, training on the pre-processed data set has a higher false negative rate for the advantaged racial category.

Figure 6.2 displays the overall prediction accuracy of the algorithm when it is trained with each of the three data sets. As shown in the figure, the best predictive accuracy is obtained from the baseline data set. Predictive information is lost both when race is redacted and when the data set is pre-processed to require independence between race and predictors. However, we see that redacting race induces a much larger performance penalty than does the pre-processed data set.

Taken together, Figures 6.1 and 6.2 suggest that pre-processing the data may result in desirable performance and equity trade-offs. In particular, pre-processing enforces statistical parity at a marginal performance cost. Although there is a discrepancy across racial groups with respect to false negative rates, we make three observations. First, it is not possible to attain statistical parity while balancing false negative rates (see Chapter Four for further details). Second, the absolute discrepancy in false negative rates between the two racial groups is smallest using the pre-processed data. Finally, pre-processing results in a lower false negative rate for the disadvantaged racial group than for the advantaged racial group, shifting the burden of false negatives from disadvantaged to advantaged groups. This racial discrepancy in error rates may be preferred to the opposite, especially if it is an institutional priority to minimize negative outcomes of policy changes on disadvantaged groups.

FIGURE 6.2

Overall Accuracy (Pr($\hat{Y} = Y$)) for Each Pre-Processing Method

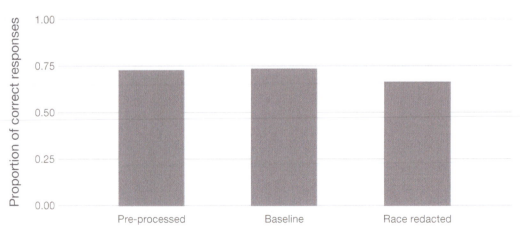

Post-Processing Interventions

Figures 6.3–6.5 summarize the consequences of several post-processing methods applied to the original hypothetical algorithm. For all methods, results reflect post-processing the output of the algorithm trained using the full baseline data set without any pre-processing. Figure 6.3 summarizes the equity properties resulting from several post-processing methods (these methods are described in further detail in Appendixes A and B). The left panel of Figure 6.3 shows that although the baseline algorithm predicts promotions at higher rates for the advantaged racial group, several post-processing methods reduce this discrepancy. As expected, the statistical parity post-processing method attains nearly exact statistical parity; the advantaged and disadvantaged racial groups are predicted to be promoted at nearly the same rate. The equalized odds and equalized opportunity methods, though not designed explicitly to attain statistical parity, also greatly reduce the baseline discrepancy in promotion rates. Interestingly, applying equalized error rate post-processing seems to exacerbate the baseline discrepancy. The right panel of Figure 6.3 shows that the baseline algorithm has higher false negative rates for the disadvantaged racial group, which are nearly elimi-

FIGURE 6.3

Equity Measures Compared Across Racial Categories for Each Post-Processing Method

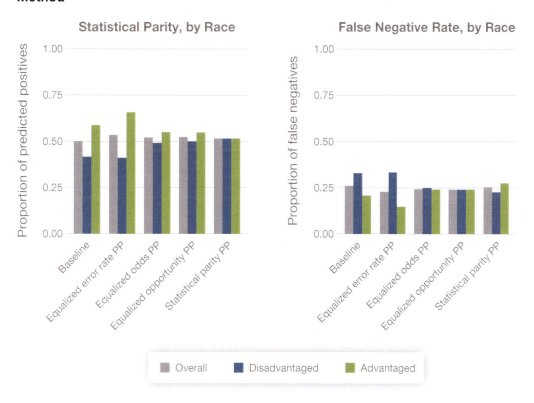

NOTE: PP = post-processing. The left panel shows a comparison of the proportion of positives predicted ($\hat{Y} = 1$) for each racial category, and the right panel shows a comparison of the false negative rates for each racial category.

nated by equalized odds and equalized opportunity post-processing. This is to be expected, because both post-processing methods are designed to equalize false negative rates across racial groups. Although statistical parity post-processing is not explicitly designed to equalize false negative rates, we also see that the discrepancy observed in the baseline model is greatly reduced after it is applied. The slight discrepancy in false negative rates that persists reverses the baseline scenario; after statistical parity is enforced, false negative rates are slightly higher for the advantaged racial group. Equalized error rate post-processing actually widens the disparity observed in the baseline, resulting in even higher false negative rates for the disadvantaged racial class. It is notable, however, that equalized error rate post-processing attains the lowest population-wide false negative rate.

Although there are significant differences observed between the various post-processing methods with respect to equity, Figure 6.4 demonstrates that all of the methods are virtually indistinguishable with respect to overall performance (by a slim margin, statistical parity post-processing has the worst overall accuracy). Taken together, Figures 6.3 and 6.4 suggest that the equity gains provided by equalized odds, equalized opportunity, and statistical parity post-processing can be attained without substantially diminishing predictive performance. Although this holds in our simulated case, it may not be (and often will not be) the case in a real application, and performance will need to be balanced against equity goals.

Finally, Figure 6.5 displays the different thresholds applied to each racial category by each post-processing method. Recall that post-processing methods identify race-specific thresholds to minimize differential performance across race with respect to a specific metric (see Appendix B). The baseline method applies the same threshold regardless of race when predicting promotion selection decisions. As shows in Figure 6.5, equalized odds, equalized opportunity, and statistical parity post-processing each require that the threshold for pre-

FIGURE 6.4

Overall Accuracy (Pr($\hat{Y}$ = Y)) for Each Post-Processing Method

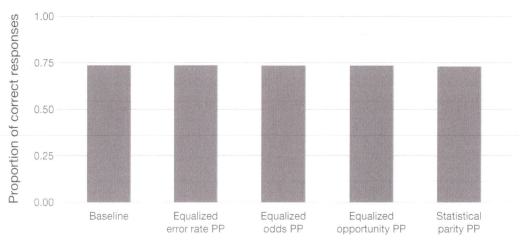

NOTE: PP = post-processing.

FIGURE 6.5

Race-Specific Thresholds Identified for Each Post-Processing Method

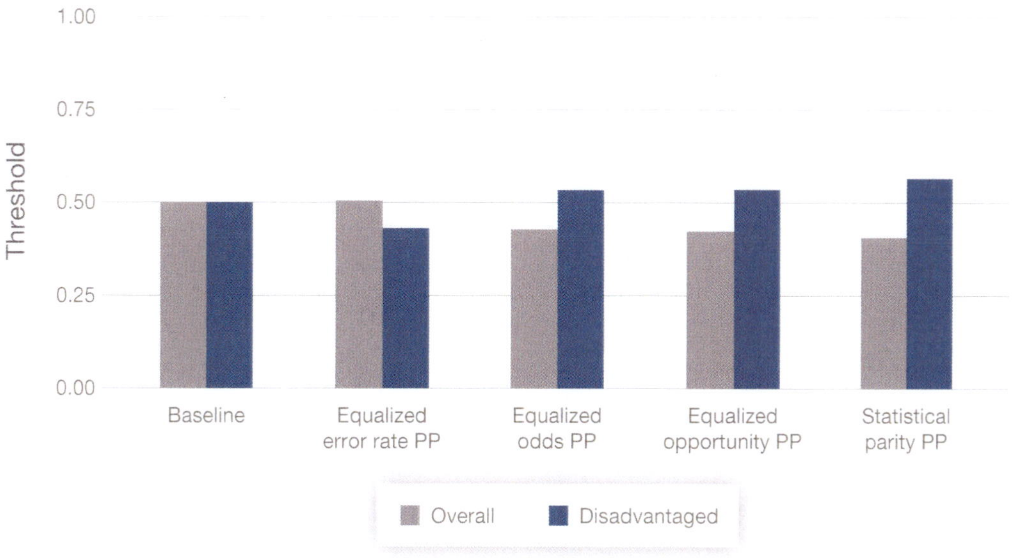

NOTE: PP = post-processing.

dicted promotion is lower for the disadvantaged racial group and higher for the advantaged racial group. Conversely, the equalized error rate post-processing actually results in a lower threshold for the advantaged group.

Intuitively, different thresholds across different racial groups connote different standards applied to different racial groups. This may not necessarily be a fair interpretation of differential thresholds. For instance, consider a situation in which the eligible populations in each racial group were equally qualified for promotion, but historical discriminatory practices resulted in fewer promotions among the disadvantaged group. In practice, then, the historical patterns of promotions required *higher* standards for the disadvantaged group relative to the advantaged group. Within the historical data, we would see that an individual from the disadvantaged group would have a lower predicted probability of promotion than a comparable member of the advantaged group. In this hypothetical situation, lowering the probability threshold via statistical parity post-processing would actually correct the observed historical discrimination.

Summary

Because the hypothetical promotion selection prediction algorithm is used in high-stakes, individual-level decisions, it poses a high equity risk. We argue that the overarching military priorities can be translated into mathematical equity concepts of fairness through unawareness, false negative rate balance, and statistical parity. After considering several algorithm modifications, including pre- and post-processing, we found that several interventions yielded substantial equity benefits over the baseline with negligible overall performance impact. Particularly promising approaches were (1) data pre-processing using the method from Johndrow and Lum, 2019, (2) statistical parity post-processing, (3) equal opportunity post-processing, and (4) equalized odds post processing. Simply redacting race, in this example, resulted in worse overall performance without substantially mitigating racial equity concerns observed in the baseline model. We emphasize that these findings are not meant to serve as general suggestions but instead reflect the results of a hypothetical case study. Different methodologies may be better suited in real-world applications with alternative equity priorities.

CHAPTER SEVEN

Conclusions

We conclude this report with some recommendations for policymakers at DoD who wish to promote equity for their personnel and for researchers who seek to develop ML applications as aids to decisionmaking processes.

Recommendations

Recommendation 1: Audit Algorithms That Pose an Equity Risk

Algorithms that are used to aid high-stakes decisions about individuals must be audited to ensure they are meeting the equity goals for their particular application. This includes auditing both the performance properties of algorithms and the data used to train them. The RAND Algorithmic Equity Tool developed with this report offers a way to assess the equity of the predictions made by an ML algorithm. It also allows users to make pre-processing or post-processing adjustments to algorithms that guarantee certain types of fairness. Lastly, the RAND Algorithmic Equity Tool allows users to weigh the equity and non-equity trade-offs that result from modifications to enhance equity. Practitioners who are developing algorithms for specific applications to be used as part of a decisionmaking process can use this tool to evaluate their algorithms.

Recommendation 2: Increase Specificity of Equity Priorities

Both auditing and enforcing equity priorities in ML algorithms necessitate translating those priorities into concrete, mathematical concepts. Current DoD equity policies typically lack adequate specificity to perform this translation. We recommend that DoD consider moving toward more concrete language in specifying its equity goals. To do so, DoD should consider adopting equity definitions developed by the algorithmic fairness literature.

Although we sought in this report to draw connections between current DoD policies and technical definitions of equity, policymakers should aim to make these connections explicit. This would enable those who are creating decision-aiding algorithms to know what equity norms they need to meet, and it would inhibit downstream consequences that conflict with the desired policy goals. Defining these equity goals may be challenging for DoD, given the varying opinions and potential trade-offs, but providing clear goals that can be matched to technical definitions would increase the development of equitable ML algorithms to help streamline personnel management decisions.

Recommendation 3: Consider Using Machine Learning as an Aid to Human Personnel Management Decisions

Although ML algorithms threaten to introduce algorithmic bias, we do not believe that the alternative of human-only decisions is preferable. The ability to both audit and constrain an ML algorithm to meet equity priorities is a considerable strength over a human-only decision process. Although human-only processes can and should be audited, it is far more difficult to adjust subjective human decisions to meet equity priorities than it is to enforce equity criteria on algorithmic predictions. We believe that, if implemented carefully, ML algorithms have the opportunity to offer a more objective and more equitable decision process. In addition to the potential equity advantages of ML algorithms, arguably the most significant advantages relate to non-equity considerations. ML algorithms are capable of leveraging far more data to derive their predictions than humans can, and such algorithms have the potential to automate otherwise laborious processes.

Overview of Technical Equity Definitions

In this appendix, we describe some standard equity definitions from the algorithmic fairness literature. Each equity definition requires an algorithm to have identical performance properties across levels of the protected variable with respect to a particular performance measure. Various equity definitions differ from one another in their choice of performance measure. When the predicted outcome is binary (as is the case for all examples we consider in this report), the various performance measures are standard statistical concepts: false positive rates, positive predictive value, etc.

Notation

We will use the following notations throughout this section. G denotes the protected class (which, in this report, will indicate an individual's race). Y denotes the true outcome of interest, and $\hat{Y}$ refers to the algorithm's prediction of the outcome. For instance, in a recruiting application, Y may be a binary variable that indicates whether an individual truly accesses ($Y = 1$ if they do, $Y = 0$ if they do not), and $\hat{Y}$ denotes the algorithm's prediction of accession. Throughout this report, we exclusively focus on binary outcomes. Although there are extensions of all these concepts for numerical outcomes, the binary case reflects most common personnel management decisionmaking processes. We denote X to be any attributes (excluding race) that the algorithm uses to make its predictions. For instance, the ML algorithm may predict whether an individual will access based on the individual's age, gender, geographical location (all of which are included in X), and race (G). The accuracy of a predictive algorithm is determined by comparing $\hat{Y}$ (the predicted outcomes) to Y (the true outcomes). We are interested in settings in which the prediction $\hat{Y}$ is used to inform a decision.

Equity Definitions

We follow the equity framework of Barocas, Hardt, and Narayanan, 2019, and consider three broad classes of equity definitions: independence, separation, and sufficiency. Technically speaking, these three classes of definitions have to do with statistical independence relationships between the outcome Y, the predictions $\hat{Y}$, and the protected class G. The basic properties of these definitions are summarized in Table A.1.

TABLE A.1
Summary of the Classes of Equity Measures

Independence	Separation	Sufficiency
$\hat{Y} \perp G$	$\hat{Y} \perp G \mid Y$	$Y \perp G \mid \hat{Y}$

NOTE: $\perp$ indicates the variables are independent of one another.

Independence Definitions of Equity

The independence class of equity definitions require that the predicted outcomes $\hat{Y}$ are distributed similarly across different levels of the protected attribute G. The most common such definition is that of *statistical parity*, which, for the case of a binary outcome and binary protected attribute, is met if the following condition holds:

$$P(\hat{Y} = 1 \mid G = 1) = P(\hat{Y} = 1 \mid G = 0).$$

A less rigid variant of statistical parity is referred to as *limited disparate impact*, which requires only approximately equal distributions across the protected class. For the case of a binary outcome and binary protected attribute, limited disparate impact may take the following form:

$$0.8P(\hat{Y} = 1 \mid G = 1) \leq P(\hat{Y} = 1 \mid G = 0).$$

This expression requires that the rate of positive predictions for the disadvantaged race or ethnicity ($G = 0$) is at least 80 percent that of the advantaged race or ethnicity ($G = 1$). This condition follows what is sometimes referred to as the 80 percent rule (Feldman et al., 2015). This formulation of limited disparate impact treats the advantaged and disadvantaged group asymmetrically. In particular, if the advantaged group has a much lower rate of positive prediction than the disadvantaged group, limited disparate impact will hold under this definition. Alternatively, one can treat the two groups symmetrically by additionally require that

$$0.8P(\hat{Y} = 1 \mid G = 0) \leq P(\hat{Y} = 1 \mid G = 1).$$

A final version of statistical parity is known as *conditional statistical parity*, which requires equal distributions of outcomes conditional on a set of variables deemed to be legitimate:

$$P(\hat{Y} = 1 \mid G = 1, X = x) = P(\hat{Y} = 1 \mid G = 0, X = x).$$

Separation Definitions of Equity

The separation class of definitions requires that individuals with the same true outcome have similar predictions, regardless of G. When the outcome is binary, separation definitions of equity correspond to equating standard statistical measures across the protected class. For instance, false positive balance corresponds to equating false positive rates across the protected class,

$$P(\hat{Y} = 1 \mid G = 1, Y = 0) = P(\hat{Y} = 1 \mid G = 0, Y = 0)$$

and false negative balance corresponds to equating false negative rates across the protected class,

$$P(\hat{Y} = 0 | G = 1, Y = 1) = P(\hat{Y} = 0 | G = 0, Y = 1).$$

Balancing false negative rates (or, equivalently, balancing false positive rates), is sometimes referred to as *equal opportunity* (Hardt, Price and Srebro, 2016).[1] Balancing both false positives and false negatives is referred to as *equalized odds*.

Sufficiency Definitions of Equity

The sufficiency class of definitions requires that individuals with similar predictions also have similar outcomes, regardless of G. Note that this is, in a sense, the inverse of the separation definitions. Intuitively, these equity definitions are met when algorithmic predictions have the same meaning for individuals, regardless of their race. For instance, positive predictions are not more predictive of positive outcomes for one race or another. When the outcome is binary, balancing positive predictive values,

$$P(Y = 1 | G = 1, \hat{Y} = 1) = P(Y = 1 | G = 0, \hat{Y} = 1)$$

or balancing negative predictive values,

$$P(Y = 0 | G = 1, \hat{Y} = 0) = P(Y = 0 | G = 0, \hat{Y} = 0)$$

are examples of sufficiency definitions.

Although sufficiency and separation are closely related concepts, they typically are not simultaneously attainable, as is discussed below. In the context of recidivism prediction (as in the COMPAS algorithm [Angwin et al., 2016]), sufficiency is the primary concern for judges when interpreting the score to make sentencing decisions. If the predictions did not satisfy sufficiency, then a given score presented in court would correspond to different levels of evidence depending on the race or ethnicity of the defendant. In the same setting, separation may be the primary concern for defendants. From their perspective, the algorithm would be considered unfair if Black individuals were more likely to receive positive recidivism predictions than White individuals among the population of individuals who truly do not recidivate.

Other Definitions of Equity

The notion of fairness through unawareness is related to a more general class of fairness concepts that are collectively referred to as *similarity-based* definitions (Dwork et al., 2012). The general concept behind all these definitions is that individuals who are similar across all nonprotected attributes (e.g., X_{-G}) should have similar outcomes. This definition of fairness is often referred to as *individual fairness*.

Another broad literature on fairness metrics concerns *causal-based* definitions, which are grounded in a more sophisticated causal framework (Coston et al., 2020; Mishler, Kennedy, and Chouldechova, 2021). These definitions may be preferred in settings in which the labeling of data used to train the algorithm is believed to be subject to racial biases.

---

[1] Although the term is *equal opportunity*, this definition is not explicitly connected to equal opportunity as defined by the EEOC.

Table A.2 provides a summary of the equity definitions discussed in this appendix.

Incompatibility of Equity Definitions

There is a large literature documenting the mutual incompatibility of various fairness definitions (Berk et al., 2021; Chouldechova, 2017; Dwork et al., 2012; Kleinberg, 2018). Under weak assumptions, it can be shown that independence, separation, and sufficiency are all pairwise-conflicting (e.g., independence and separation are not simultaneously attainable). Perhaps the most well-studied case is the incompatibility between calibration and equalized odds; the contradiction between these two fairness metrics was central to the debate surrounding the COMPAS recidivism risk score (Angwin et al., 2016). Although calibration and equalized odds are incompatible with each other, it is also generally true that calibration and equalized odds are both separately incompatible with statistical parity. Furthermore, statistical parity is known to conflict with individual fairness (Dwork et al., 2012).

TABLE A.2
Equity Definitions

Name	Definition
Independence definitions	
Statistical parity	$P\left(\hat{Y} = 1 \mid G = 0\right) = P\left(\hat{Y} = 1 \mid G = 1\right)$
Limited disparate impact (asymmetric)	$0.8P(Y = 1 \mid G = 1) \leq P(Y = 1 \mid G = 0)$
Limited disparate impact (symmetric)	$0.8P(Y = 1 \mid G = 1) \leq P(Y = 1 \mid G = 0)$ $0.8P(Y = 1 \mid G = 0) \leq P(Y = 1 \mid G = 1)$
Conditional statistical parity	$P\left(\hat{Y} = 1 \mid G = 0, X = x\right) = P\left(\hat{Y} = 1 \mid G = 1, X = x\right)$
Separation definitions	
False positive balance	$P\left(\hat{Y} = 1 \mid Y = 0, G = g\right) = P\left(\hat{Y} = 1 \mid Y = 0\right)$
False negative balance	$P\left(\hat{Y} = 0 \mid Y = 1, G = g\right) = P\left(\hat{Y} = 0 \mid Y = 1\right)$
Equalized Odds	False positive balance and false negative balance
Sufficiency definitions	
Positive predictive value balance	$P\left(Y = 1 \mid \hat{Y} = 1, G = g\right) = P\left(Y = 1 \mid \hat{Y} = 1\right)$
Negative predictive value balance	$P\left(Y = 0 \mid \hat{Y} = 0, G = g\right) = P\left(Y = 0 \mid \hat{Y} = 0\right)$
Conditional use accuracy equality	Positive predictive value balance and negative predictive value balance
Other definitions	
Equalized accuracy	$P\left(\hat{Y} = Y \mid G = g\right) = P\left(\hat{Y} = Y\right)$
Fairness through unawareness	$\hat{Y} = f(X_{\iota})$
Similarity-based definitions	(From Dwork et al., 2012) $D(M(X), M(X')) \leq d(X, X')$

Technical Description of Post-Processing Methods

In this report, we implement a simple post-processing procedure that is applicable to virtually any equity concept in the binary classification setting. We assume that the baseline predictive algorithm produces predicted probabilities p_i for each individual, corresponding to an estimated probability that $Y_i = 1$. Binary estimates $\hat{Y}_i$ are obtained by assigning $\hat{Y}_i = 1$ if p_i is greater than a threshold θ. Our procedure seeks optimal thresholds, which typically differ across levels of the protected class G, that are intended to minimize differential performance while optimizing overall performance. For a protected variable G with two levels, we solve the optimization problem

$$\underset{(\theta_0, \theta_1)}{\text{minimize}} \ (\text{Equity Penalty}) + (\text{Accuracy Penalty}),$$

where θ_0 and θ_1 are the thresholds for the disadvantaged and advantaged class, respectively. In the above optimization, we define the accuracy penalty to be $P(\hat{Y} \neq Y)$, which is one minus the overall observed accuracy of the predictive algorithm. We define the equity penalty to be the absolute value of the difference in performance between the two groups, where performance is defined by an appropriate metric. For instance, if we seek to equalize false negatives, then

$$\text{Equity Penalty} = \left| P(\hat{Y} = 0 \mid Y = 1, G = 0) - P(\hat{Y} = 0 \mid Y = 1, G = 1) \right|,$$

which is estimated from the observed data. Using this approach, the provided tool is capable of enforcing statistical parity, false negative balance, equalized odds, positive predictive value balance, and equalized accuracy. For equalized odds, the equity penalty is the sum of the equity penalties corresponding to false positive balance and false negative balance.

Machine Learning in the Department of Defense for Nonpersonnel Issues

Although military equity concerns lie primarily in personnel decisions, the use of ML may raise ethical questions in a wide variety of domains, such as improving situational awareness and decisionmaking in the military context, increasing the safety of operating equipment, and implementing predictive maintenance and supply. On these matters, DoD has laid out an AI strategy that includes a call for ethical and responsible use of AI by DoD (DoD, 2019). DoD states that it is not just interested in using AI to remain globally competitive but that it also wants to be a leader in the ethical use of AI and partner with leading academics and practitioners outside the military. The Air Force has echoed these same ideas in its supplementary AI strategy document, signaling a commitment to increase public trust and transparency in the ethical use of AI throughout its five focus points (Department of the Air Force, 2019). Various reports have been developed by DoD, partners, or federally funded research and development centers that consider the use of AI by DoD.

The Joint Artificial Intelligence Center (JAIC) was created to handle matters of deploying AI for DoD, and it has released ethical principles for AI (JAIC, undated). The five principles adopted were that AI should be responsible, equitable, traceable, reliable, and governable. Each of these principles relates to matters of diversity and fairness indirectly, but the second directly states, "The Department will take deliberate steps to minimize unintended bias in AI capabilities" (JAIC, 2020a, p. 4). The JAIC expands on this principle by stating that DoD should "account for statistical, social, and human bias," "identify entry points for bias and interject controls to measure/mitigate/test for bias throughout the lifecycle," "consider how other actors may use the data or model which may lead to unintended outcomes," and perform "rigorous testing aimed at reducing risk, bias, and harm reduction" (JAIC, 2020a, p. 4).

The policies take on additional meaning when viewed through different applications of ML or artificial intelligence. For example, much of DoD's AI work has focused on the use of autonomous weapons systems and other applications in warfare and defense. In this context, the goal may be to minimize racial bias in surveillance programs or protect against unintended consequences when using autonomous weapons systems. In the context of personnel management, algorithms may be constructed to improve processes, such as promotion selection decisions, but these algorithms should be monitored for bias and tested to ensure they are working fairly.

There are equity concerns in regard to DoD's use of ML outside personnel management. Previous work, such as Morgan et al., 2020, considers the benefits and ethical risks in military applications in the use of automated weapon systems and intelligence and surveillance. Although these applications do not involve personnel management, they often have direct or indirect impacts on individuals, and the consequences may be distributed unequally across sensitive attributes. For example, it is possible for surveillance or autonomous weapons to have differential performance properties across race or ethnicity, a circumstance that may not be considered fair or desirable.

The technological edge from ML has the potential to boost national security, since well-designed ML systems can detect targets or predict maintenance issues at faster rates than humans, especially compared to less experienced humans. Reducing personnel has its advantages in the field by reducing the number of fighters that have to be placed in a potentially life-threatening situation. With an ML system making decisions, less experienced personnel might be left to manage the system, freeing up more-experienced personnel to perform more-complex decisions and tasks. ML systems can also assist with rescue operations, since unmanned systems can be developed to go into areas that humans probably could not.

The greater complexity ML introduces carries with it more-nuanced risks. As ML systems get more complex, unexpected failures or interactions unforeseen in the original design, especially in relation to ML systems interacting with each other, may become harder to diagnose and preempt. The increased speed of automated decisionmaking may make conflicts escalate more rapidly. Replacing a human system with an ML system also creates a perceived "moral buffer." Because an ML system makes decisions using existing data, any system failure that leads to unethical outcomes creates uncertainty as to how to remedy the situation, since no one person can easily be held morally or legally responsible for the decisions of a machine. These complexities may require that human managers of the system undergo extensive training, which may negate some of the potential benefits. In addition to privacy concerns and fears of implementing a system that relatively few people can understand, there are issues that plague any software, including issues that result from software bugs, adversaries successfully attacking the system, and the fear of data feeding into the machine being poisoned in any way.

Prior Work Using Machine Learning for Nonpersonnel Decisionmaking

In this section, we describe the primary areas of ML application within the national security space beyond personnel management. We discuss applications that are currently deployed, as well as applications for which there is ongoing investment and development. Our literature review consisted of (1) a systematic review of all RAND projects developed from 2017 to 2021 in the national security divisions and (2) a review of research external to RAND that was identified within RAND work. Our review is designed to reflect the applications within

DoD and the Department of Homeland Security. Other work provides more-detailed overviews of the breadth of ML applications in the military and other areas of interest in relation to national security. Not all of these applications of ML pose an equity risk, but we aim to provide a brief overview of all categories to convey the breadth of ML in national security.

Unmanned Systems

Unmanned systems are a large area of development in national security that is increasingly attempting to incorporate ML into technology. Most development lies in unmanned aerial systems, but there has been growing investment by the Navy to developed unmanned submarines and other submersible systems (Trevithick, 2020). There has been significant progress made in such programs as Skyborg, an autonomous capability that the Air Force seeks to implement on low-cost aircraft to assist with decisionmaking (Air Force Research Laboratory, undated).

Intelligence, Surveillance, Reconnaissance

There is much interest in integrating ML—particularly, Computer Vision technologies—to improve intelligence, surveillance, and reconnaissance (ISR) operations. Raytheon is investing in this space with such projects as Cognitive Aids to Sensor Processing, Exploration and Response (CASPER), a software program that interprets operator requests to control sensor and data processing functions. Jim Wright from Raytheon envisions CASPER to perform such tasks as scanning "for fast boats and prioritiz[ing] by threat to the carrier" (Raytheon Intelligence and Space, 2020). In 2020, Lockheed Martin demonstrated an ISR capability in an ML algorithm that was able to detect, identify, and capture an image of a target (Helfrich, 2020). In the Army, facial recognition technology is being actively pursued to assist with ISR with U.S. Central Command and the Combined Joint Task Force. Operation Inherent Resolve already uses these technologies (Williams, 2019).

Humanitarian Assistance and Disaster Relief

There is increasing interest in the military for incorporation of ML in disaster relief operations. Most of these projects incorporate ML via detection and monitoring to assist in evacuating residents. The main examples of such projects are Fireline (JAIC, 2019), which is being developed to detect and communicate wildfires, and Floodline (JAIC, 2020b), which is being developed to monitor and detect changing water levels for preventing flood damage and rescuing people. Both of these projects are being developed by the JAIC and partnering organizations. Another example of ML use in disaster relief operations is AUDREY (Seffers, 2015), an ML tool being developed with the Department of Homeland Security and the National Aeronautics and Space Administration's (NASA's) Jet Propulsion Laboratory to combine and synthesize information from multiple channels to ease the cognitive load that first responders face during emergencies.

Command and Control

ML has been identified in some studies for potential support of command and control (C2). Lingel et al., 2020, summarizes many such applications. For example, ML could enable distributed C2, which is designated as a desire by the Air Force, by prioritizing communications between nodes. This would allow less experienced staff to complete planning activities, freeing up more-experienced staff for more-complex operations. Other examples include using Computer Vision to process multisource intelligence and perform data fusion, using expert systems to flag potential conflicts and opportunities, and using natural language processing to provide text recommendations (Lingel et al., 2020). An ML application used for enemy force suppression could also be combined with C2 in a surface-to-air missile scenario, especially in regard to resource selection and play recommendations (Lingel et al., 2020). Lastly, ML methods could be incorporated in simulating such scenarios to further inform decisions in regard to hypothetical scenarios.

Conclusion

This report focuses on the personnel space, where DoD has emphasized both equity priorities and ML development. However, there is considerable development and deployment of ML outside the personnel space, where DoD has few or no expressed equity policies. Some of these areas of ML development involve high-stakes decisions about individuals, such as ML applications for surveillance and autonomous weapons. DoD should articulate equity guidelines in all areas in which ML development occurs.

References

Air Force Instruction 36-7001, *Diversity & Inclusion*, Washington, D.C.: Department of the Air Force, February 19, 2019. As of August 17, 2022:
https://www.af.mil/Portals/1/documents/diversity/1/afi36-7001.pdf

Air Force Research Laboratory, "Skyborg," webpage, undated. As of August 26, 2022:
https://afresearchlab.com/technology/vanguards/successstories/skyborg

Amazon, "How We Hire and Develop the Best Talent at Amazon," webpage, undated. As of August 17, 2022:
https://www.aboutamazon.com/news/workplace/hiring-the-best-talent

Angwin, Julia, Jeff Larson, Surya Mattu, and Lauren Kirchner, "Machine Bias," *ProPublica*, May 23, 2016. As of August 17, 2022:
https://www.propublica.org/article/machine-bias-risk-assessments-in-criminal-sentencing

Arrieta, Alejandro Barredo, Natalia Díaz-Rodríguez, Javier Del Ser, Adrien Bennetot, Siham Tabik, Alberto Barbado, Salvador Garcia, Sergio Gil-Lopez, Daniel Molina, Richard Benjamins, Raja Chatila, and Francisco Herrera, "Explainable Artificial Intelligence (XAI): Concepts, Taxonomies, Opportunities and Challenges Toward Responsible AI," *Information Fusion*, Vol. 58, June 2020, pp. 82–115.

Barocas, Solon, Moritz Hardt, and Arvind Narayanan, *Fairness and Machine Learning*, fairmlbook.org, 2019. As of August 17, 2022:
https://fairmlbook.org/

Berk, Richard, Hoda Heidari, Shahin Jabbari, Michael Kearns, and Aaron Roth, "Fairness in Criminal Justice Risk Assessments: The State of the Art," *Sociological Methods & Research*, Vol. 50, No. 1, February 2021, pp. 3–44.

Chouldechova, Alexandra, "Fair Prediction with Disparate Impact: A Study of Bias in Recidivism Prediction Instruments," *Big Data*, Vol. 5, No. 2, June 2017, pp. 153–163.

Chouldechova, Alexandra, Emily Putnam-Hornstein, Diana Benavides-Prado, Oleksandr Fialko, and Rhema Vaithianathan, "A Case Study of Algorithm-Assisted Decision Making in Child Maltreatment Hotline Screening Decisions," *Proceedings of the 1st Conference on Fairness, Accountability and Transparency*, Vol. 81, New York, February 2018, pp. 134–148.

Corbett-Davies, Sam, Emma Pierson, Avi Feller, Sharad Goel, and Aziz Huq, "Algorithmic Decision Making and the Cost of Fairness," *Proceedings of the 23rd ACM SIGKDD International Conference on Knowledge Discovery and Data Mining*, Halifax, Canada: Association for Computing Machinery, August 2017, pp. 797–806.

Coston, Amanda, Alan Mishler, Edward H. Kennedy, and Alexandra Chouldechova, "Counterfactual Risk Assessments, Evaluation, and Fairness," *Proceedings of the 2020 Conference on Fairness, Accountability, and Transparency*, Barcelona, Spain: Association for Computing Machinery, January 2020, pp. 582–593.

Damberg, Cheryl L., Marc N. Elliott, and Brett A. Ewing, "Pay-For-Performance Schemes That Use Patient and Provider Categories Would Reduce Payment Disparities," *Health Affairs*, Vol. 34, No. 1, January 2015, pp. 134–142.

Dastin, Jeffrey, "Amazon Scraps Secret AI Recruiting Tool That Showed Bias Against Women," Reuters, October 10, 2018. As of August 17, 2022: https://www.reuters.com/article/us-amazon-com-jobs-automation-insight/ amazon-scraps-secret-ai-recruiting-tool-that-showed-bias-against-women-idUSKCN1MK08G

DBDI—*See* U.S. Department of Defense Board on Diversity and Inclusion.

Department of Defense Directive 1020.02E, *Diversity Management and Equal Opportunity in the DoD, Washington*, D.C.: U.S. Department of Defense, incorporating Change 2, June 1, 2018.

Department of the Air Force, "The United States Air Force Artificial Intelligence Annex to the Department of Defense Artificial Intelligence Strategy," 2019. As of August 17, 2022: https://www.af.mil/Portals/1/documents/5/USAF-AI-Annex-to-DoD-AI-Strategy.pdf

Department of the Air Force Inspector General, *Report of Inquiry (S8918P): Independent Racial Disparity Review*, December 2020. As of August 17, 2022: https://www.af.mil/Portals/1/documents/ig/IRDR.pdf

Dickstein, Corey, "Pentagon Considers Redacting Names from Promotion Packets After Removing Photos," *Stars and Stripes*, July 17, 2020. As of August 17, 2022: https://www.stripes.com/theaters/us/pentagon-considers-redacting-names-from-promotion-packets-after-removing-photos-1.637967

DoD—*See* U.S. Department of Defense.

Dwork, Cynthia, Moritz Hardt, Toniann Pitassi, Omer Reingold, and Richard Zemel, "Fairness Through Awareness," *Proceedings of the 3rd Innovations in Theoretical Computer Science Conference*, Cambridge, Mass.: Association for Computing Machinery, January 2012, pp. 214–226.

Feldman, Michael, Sorelle A. Friedler, John Moeller, Carlos Scheidegger, and Suresh Venkatasubramanian, "Certifying and Removing Disparate Impact," *Proceedings of the 21st ACM SIGKDD International Conference on Knowledge Discovery and Data Mining*, Sydney: Association for Computing Machinery, August 2015, pp. 259–268.

GCN, "Data-Driven Talent Management," December 9, 2020. As of August 17, 2022: https://gcn.com/articles/2020/12/09/army-talent-management-data-science.aspx

Goodman, Rachel, "Why Amazon's Automated Hiring Tool Discriminated Against Women," American Civil Liberties Union, blog, October 12, 2018. As of August 17, 2022: https://www.aclu.org/blog/womens-rights/womens-rights-workplace/ why-amazons-automated-hiring-tool-discriminated-against

Hardt, Moritz, Eric Price, and Nathan Srebro, "Equality of Opportunity in Supervised Learning," arXiv, October 11, 2016.

Hartnett, Gavin S., Lance Menthe, Jasmin Léveillé, Damien Baveye, Li Ang Zhang, Dara Gold, Jeff Hagen, and Jia Xu, *Operationally Relevant Artificial Training for Machine Learning: Improving the Performance of Automated Target Recognition Systems*, Santa Monica, Calif.: RAND Corporation, RR-A683-1, 2020. As of August 17, 2022: https://www.rand.org/pubs/research_reports/RRA683-1.html

Headquarters, Department of the Army, *United States Army Diversity Roadmap*, December 2010. As of August 17, 2022: https://www.armydiversity.army.mil/document/Diversity_Roadmap.pdf

Heckman, Jory, "Army Builds Retention Prediction Model Using Machine Learning," *Federal News Network*, November 11, 2020. As of August 17, 2022:
https://federalnewsnetwork.com/artificial-intelligence/2020/11/army-builds-retention-prediction-model-using-machine-learning/

Helfrich, Emma, "AI-Powered ISR Capability Introduced by Lockheed Martin," *Military Embedded Systems*, May 7, 2020. As of August 17, 2022:
https://militaryembedded.com/ai/machine-learning/ai-powered-isr-capability-introduced-by-lockheed-martin

JAIC—*See* Joint Artificial Intelligence Center.

Johndrow, James E., and Kristian Lum, "An Algorithm for Removing Sensitive Information: Application to Race-Independent Recidivism Prediction," *Annals of Applied Statistics*, Vol. 13, No. 1, March 2019, pp. 189–220.

Joint Artificial Intelligence Center, "Ethical Principles for Artificial Intelligence," undated. As of August 17, 2022:
https://www.ai.mil/docs/Ethical_Principles_for_Artificial_Intelligence.pdf

———, "The JAIC Is Supporting National Guard Efforts to Combat Destructive Wildfires," *AI in Defense*, blog, October 1, 2019. As of August 17, 2022:
https://www.ai.mil/blog_09_16_19.html

———, "Department of Defense Joint Artificial Intelligence Center Responsible AI Champions Pilot," 2020a. As of September 9, 2022:
https://www.ai.mil/docs/08_21_20_responsible_ai_champions_pilot.pdf

———, "DoD AI in Disaster Response Demonstrates Progress, Promise for Future," *AI in Defense*, blog, January 31, 2020b. As of August 17, 2022:
https://www.ai.mil/blog_01_31_20-dod-ai-hadr-in-disaster-response-demonstrates-progress.html

Kamarck, Kristy N., *Diversity, Inclusion, and Equal Opportunity in the Armed Services: Background and Issues for Congress*, Washington, D.C.: Congressional Research Service, R44321, June 5, 2019.

Keller, Kirsten M., Maria C. Lytell, David Schulker, Kimberly Curry Hall, Louis T. Mariano, John S. Crown, Miriam Matthews, Brandon Crosby, Lisa Saum-Manning, Douglas Yeung, Leslie Adrienne Payne, Felix Knutson, and Leann Caudill, *Advancement and Retention Barriers in the U.S. Air Force Civilian White Collar Workforce: Implications for Demographic Diversity*, Santa Monica, Calif.: RAND Corporation, RR-2643-AF, 2020. As of August 17, 2022:
https://www.rand.org/pubs/research_reports/RR2643.html

Kleinberg, Jon, "Inherent Trade-Offs in Algorithmic Fairness," ACM SIGMETRICS Performance Evaluation Review, Vol. 46, No. 1, June 2018, p. 40.

Kriner, Douglas L., and Francis X. Shen, "Invisible Inequality: The Two Americas of Military Sacrifice," *University of Memphis Law Review*, Vol. 46, August 2016, pp. 545–635.

Lim, Nelson, Michelle Cho, and Kimberly Curry Hall, *Planning for Diversity: Options and Recommendations for DoD Leaders*, Santa Monica, Calif.: RAND Corporation, MG-743-OSD, 2008. As of August 17, 2022:
https://www.rand.org/pubs/monographs/MG743.html

Lim, Nelson, Louis T. Mariano, Amy G. Cox, David Schulker, and Lawrence M. Hanser, *Improving Demographic Diversity in the U.S. Air Force Officer Corps*, Santa Monica, Calif.: RAND Corporation, RR-495-AF, 2014. As of August 17, 2022:
https://www.rand.org/pubs/research_reports/RR495.html

Lingel, Sherrill, Jeff Hagen, Eric Hastings, Mary Lee, Matthew Sargent, Matthew Walsh, Li Ang Zhang, and David Blancett, *Joint All-Domain Command and Control for Modern Warfare: An Analytic Framework for Identifying and Developing Artificial Intelligence Applications*, Santa Monica, Calif.: RAND Corporation, RR-4408/1-AF, 2020. As of August 17, 2022: https://www.rand.org/pubs/research_reports/RR4408z1.html

Lipton, Zachary C., "The Mythos of Model Interpretability," *Queue*, Vol. 16, No. 3, May–June 2018, pp. 31–57.

Military Leadership Diversity Commission, *Decision Paper #8: Metrics*, Arlington, Va., February 2011. As of August 17, 2022: https://diversity.defense.gov/Portals/51/Documents/Resources/Commission/docs/Decision%20 Papers/Paper%208%20-%20Metrics.pdf

Miller, Christopher C., Acting Secretary of Defense, "Actions to Improve Racial and Ethnic Diversity and Inclusion in the U~S. Military," memorandum for senior Pentagon leadership, commanders of the combatant commands, and defense agency and DoD field activity directors, Washington, D.C., December 17, 2020. As of August 17, 2022: https://media.defense.gov/2020/Dec/18/2002554854/-1/-1/0/ACTIONS-TO-IMPROVE-RACIAL-AND-ETHNIC-DIVERSITY-AND-INCLUSION-IN-THE-U.S.-MILITARY.PDF

Mishler, Alan, Edward H. Kennedy, and Alexandra Chouldechova, "Fairness in Risk Assessment Instruments: Post-Processing to Achieve Counterfactual Equalized Odds," *Proceedings of the 2021 ACM Conference on Fairness, Accountability, and Transparency*, Association for Computing Machinery, March 2021, pp. 386–400.

Morgan, Forrest E., Benjamin Boudreaux, Andrew J. Lohn, Mark Ashby, Christian Curriden, Kelly Klima, and Derek Grossman, *Military Applications of Artificial Intelligence: Ethical Concerns in an Uncertain World*, Santa Monica, Calif.: RAND Corporation, RR-3139-1-AF, 2020. As of August 17, 2022: https://www.rand.org/pubs/research_reports/RR3139-1.html

Morral, Andrew R., Terry L. Schell, Matthew Cefalu, Jessica Hwang, and Andrew Gelman, *Sexual Assault and Sexual Harassment in the U.S. Military: Volume 5. Estimates for Installation- and Command-Level Risk of Sexual Assault and Sexual Harassment from the 2014 RAND Military Workplace Study*, Santa Monica, Calif.: RAND Corporation, RR-870/7-OSD, 2018. As of August 17, 2022: https://www.rand.org/pubs/research_reports/RR870z7.html

Obermeyer, Ziad, Brian Powers, Christine Vogeli, and Sendhil Mullainathan, "Dissecting Racial Bias in an Algorithm Used to Manage the Health of Populations," *Science*, Vol. 366, No. 6464, October 2019, pp. 447–453.

Osoba, Osonde A., Benjamin Boudreaux, Jessica Saunders, J. Luke Irwin, Pam A. Mueller, and Samantha Cherney, *Algorithmic Equity: A Framework for Social Applications*, Santa Monica, Calif.: RAND Corporation, RR-2708-RC, 2019. As of September 9, 2022: https://www.rand.org/pubs/research_reports/RR2708.html

Public Law 112-239, National Defense Authorization Act for Fiscal Year 2013, January 2, 2013.

Raytheon Intelligence and Space, "How Artificial Intelligence and Machine Learning Will Make ISR Faster," *Breaking Defense*, September 14, 2020. As of August 17, 2022: https://breakingdefense.com/2020/09/how-artificial-intelligence-and-machine-learning-will-make-isr-faster/

Saleiro, Pedro, Benedict Kuester, Loren Hinkson, Jesse London, Abby Stevens, Ari Anisfeld, Kit T. Rodolfa, and Rayid Ghani, "Aequitas: A Bias and Fairness Audit Toolkit," ArXiv, November 14, 2018.

Schulker, David, Lisa M. Harrington, Matthew Walsh, Sandra Kay Evans, Irineo Cabreros, Dana Udwin, Anthony Lawrence, Christopher E. Maerzluft, and Claude Messan Setodji, *Developing an Air Force Retention Early Warning System: Concept and Initial Prototype*, Santa Monica, Calif.: RAND Corporation, RR-A545-1, 2021. As of August 17, 2022:
https://www.rand.org/pubs/research_reports/RRA545-1.html

Schulker, David, Nelson Lim, Luke J. Matthews, Geoffrey E. Grimm, Anthony Lawrence, and Perry Shameem Firoz, *Can Artificial Intelligence Help Improve Air Force Talent Management? An Exploratory Application*, Santa Monica, Calif.: RAND Corporation, RR-A812-1, 2021. As of August 17, 2022:
https://www.rand.org/pubs/research_reports/RRA812-1.html

Seffers, George I., "Advancing the State of Artificial Intelligence Assistants," *SIGNAL*, September 3, 2015.

Tarraf, Danielle C., William Shelton, Edward Parker, Brien Alkire, Diana Gehlhaus, Justin Grana, Alexis Levedahl, Jasmin Léveillé, Jared Mondschein, James Ryseff, Ali Wyne, Daniel Elinoff, Edward Geist, Benjamin N. Harris, Eric Hui, Cedric Kenney, Sydne Newberry, Chandler Sachs, Peter Schirmer, Danielle Schlang, Victoria Smith, Abbie Tingstad, Padmaja Vedula, and Kristin Warren, *The Department of Defense Posture for Artificial Intelligence: Assessment and Recommendations*, Santa Monica, Calif.: RAND Corporation, RR-4229-OSD, 2019. As of August 17, 2022:
https://www.rand.org/pubs/research_reports/RR4229.html

Task Force One Navy, *Final Report: Our Navy Team—Navigating a Course to True North*, 2021.

Terry, Tara L., Jeremy M. Eckhause, Michael McGee, James H. Bigelow, and Paul Emslie, *Projecting Air Force Rated Officer Inventory Across the Total Force: Total Force Blue Line Model for Rated Officer Management*, Santa Monica, Calif.: RAND Corporation, RR-2796-AF, 2019. As of August 17, 2022:
https://www.rand.org/pubs/research_reports/RR2796.html

Tong, Patricia K., Michael G. Mattock, Beth J. Asch, James Hosek, and Felix Knutson, *Modeling Career Enlisted Aviator Retention in the U.S. Air Force*, Santa Monica, Calif.: RAND Corporation, RR-3134-AF, 2020. As of August 17, 2022:
https://www.rand.org/pubs/research_reports/RR3134.html

Trevithick, Joseph, "Snakehead Will Be the Largest Underwater Drone That U.S. Nuclear Submarines Can Deploy," *The Drive*, December 28, 2020. As of August 17, 2022:
https://www.thedrive.com/the-war-zone/38443/snakehead-will-be-the-largest-underwater-drone-that-u-s-nuclear-submarines-can-deploy

Tucker, Patrick, "The US Military Is Creating the Future of Employee Monitoring," *Defense One*, March 26, 2019. As of August 17, 2022:
https://www.defenseone.com/technology/2019/03/us-military-creating-future-employee-monitoring/155824/

U.S. Department of Defense, *Diversity and Inclusion Strategic Plan 2012–2017*, Washington, D.C., 2012. As of August 17, 2022:
https://diversity.defense.gov/Portals/51/Documents/DoD_Diversity_Strategic_Plan_%20final_as%20of%2019%20Apr%2012%5B1%5D.pdf

———, *Summary of the 2018 Department of Defense Artificial Intelligence Strategy: Harnessing AI to Advance Our Security and Prosperity*, Washington, D.C., February 2019. As of August 17, 2022:
https://media.defense.gov/2019/Feb/12/2002088963/-1/-1/1/SUMMARY-OF-DOD-AI-STRATEGY.PDF

U.S. Department of Defense Board on Diversity and Inclusion, *Recommendations to Improve Racial and Ethnic Diversity and Inclusion in the U.S. Military*, 2020. As of August 17, 2022: https://media.defense.gov/2020/Dec/18/2002554852/-1/-1/0/DOD-DIVERSITY-AND-INCLUSION-FINAL-BOARD-REPORT.PDF

U.S. Equal Employment Opportunity Commission, "Uniform Guidelines on Employment Selection Procedures," *Federal Register*, Vol. 44, No. 43, March 1979. As of August 17, 2022: https://www.eeoc.gov/laws/guidance/questions-and-answers-clarify-and-provide-common-interpretation-uniform-guidelines

U.S. Navy Chief of Naval Operations, *U.S. Navy Inclusion & Diversity*, 2020.

Walsh, Matthew, David Schulker, Nelson Lim, Albert A. Robbert, Raymond E. Conley, John S. Crown, and Christopher E. Maerzluft, *Department of the Air Force Officer Talent Management Reforms: Implications for Career Field Health and Demographic Diversity*, Santa Monica, Calif.: RAND Corporation, RR-A556-1, 2021. As of August 17, 2022: https://www.rand.org/pubs/research_reports/RRA556-1.html

Williams, Lauren C., "How the Army Is Advancing Facial Recognition Technology," *FCW*, August 30, 2019. As of August 17, 2022: https://fcw.com/2019/08/how-the-army-is-advancing-facial-recognition-technology/210992/

Zhang, Yunfeng, Q. Vera Liao, and Rachel K. E. Bellamy, "Effect of Confidence and Explanation on Accuracy and Trust Calibration in AI-Assisted Decision Making," *Proceedings of the 2020 Conference on Fairness, Accountability, and Transparency*, Barcelona, Spain: Association for Computing Machinery, January 2020, pp. 295–305.